# COUNSELING THE ALCOHOLIC

To Frank Pilecki,
Gratefully for your leadership and support. —
Joseph Perez
5 Feb '85

**Joseph F. Perez, Ph.D.**
Professor of Psychology
Westfield State College
Westfield, Massachusetts

ACCELERATED DEVELOPMENT INC.
**Publisher**
Muncie, Indiana

**Counseling the Alcoholic**

Library of Congress Catalogue Number: 84-71162

International Standard Book Number: 0-915202-51-4



Cover Design: Colleen D. Ahern

Techanical Assistants: Michelle Crowe
Tanya Dalton
Judy McWilliams
Sheila Sheward

Order additional copies from

Accelerated Development Inc.
Publishers Tel (317) 284-7511
3400 Kilgore Avenue, Muncie, Indiana 47304

**To Monique DeSantis (Mimi), finally!**

# FOREWORD I

.....after struggling for many years through endless stacks of text books, many of which, quite frankly, seeming largely like exercises in academic intellectualism, this book by Joseph Perez was handed to me and the question was asked, "Will you read this and tell me what you think?"

I have read it and I am happy to tell you what I think.

The author demonstrates that rare wisdom and ability to translate a considerable body of knowledge and experience into a concise, highly focused and refreshingly readable piece of work. His effort represents a sensitive awareness of a truly desperate need, i.e., to better know the alcoholic, to better know oneself as he/she relates to the alcoholic, and finally, to better know a few probably effective therapeutic techniques. Dr. Perez liberally documents his case with contemporary research data.

This book should find its way into the hands of every student, teacher, agency, and facility dealing with this country's growing Public Health Colossus, alcoholism.

The need is imperative.

H. Richard Doerr, M.Ed.
Alcoholism Treatment Program
Rutland Heights Hospital
Rutland, MA

# FOREWORD II

I was able to approach the manuscript *Counseling The Alcoholic,* authored by Dr. Joseph F. Perez, from three standpoints—that of recovering alcoholic, of alcohol rehabilitation counselor, and as an assistant professor with an M.A. degree (plus 30 hours) in interdisciplinary social science. I also have had eight years experience as a Massachusetts probation officer with a caseload consistently composed, in the main, of persons with alcohol and drug dependency problems.

I simply cannot, in a few words, fully convey to anyone outside the field the significance of Dr. Perez's accomplishment in compiling a book that is at once so concise and so thorough in the way it isolates and explains major issues confronting every alcoholic client and every alcohol counselor. In the sea of literature, theory, and experience that surrounds us, he has focused on the reefs and shoals that have shipwrecked all of us and given us both chart and compass to the archipelago of islands that must be visited and explored on the journey to recovery. The unique utility of the book is the manner in which it zeroes directly in on the major issues of and impediments to recovery which are universal in dealing with the disease, and I am not aware of any other publication that even attempts this goal. I must stress that the alcoholic in treatment and the counselor in the treatment setting are most often working together under very severe time limits, usually 7 to 30 days. In that short time they are dealing with a disease that has progressed unattended for years. This book is of inestimable value in helping the counselor maximize the benefit of scarce hours.

The book is constructed and written in a way that not only facilitates its reading but also compels it. Assuming the reader's goal is to develop or enhance counseling skills, the literary style and the sequence of material creates a momentum that carries one naturally to the objective.

The authenticity of the book, in the opinion of this alcoholic, is beyond question. It is all the more remarkable because Dr. Perez, not himself a victim of the disease, has entered our strange world and absorbed its essence with an empathy and understanding usually attained only by fellow-sufferers.

He has synthesized virtually all significant research into an extremely practical tool that I, personally, now regard as indispensable to my own work. Again, let me emphasize that in a market with burgeoning demand, I am not aware of any publication quite as useful, practical, and understandable.

While not by any means a "scientifically" significant experiment, I believe it is instructive to note that twice in group sessions at a short-term rehabilitation center, I focused patients on concepts contained in Dr. Perez's book. In both instances, the patients themselves became involved in discussion so animated that the groups exceeded their alloted time and had to be curtailed by me in order to stay within the program schedule.

L. Michael McCartney, M.A.
Westfield, MA

# PREFACE

This is a focused, succinct presentation. Part I treats the *alcoholic as a person and essential characteristics for understanding.* Part II deals with qualities which make for an *effective alcoholism counselor.* Part III is concerned with *selected theoretical topics* about counseling and Part IV, replete with illustrations at the end of each subject topic, deals with *practical techniques* of counseling the alcoholic. Each part contains topics for discussion and is followed with a bibliography of research cited and other traditional entries.

In sum, after reading this book the thoughtful reader will have an in-depth understanding of the dynamics of the alcoholic, will know what qualities make for an effective counselor of alcoholics, and will be knowledgeable about both the theory and practice of counseling alcoholics.

## Goals

Basic goals in writing this book were as follows:

1. To make it academically and professionally respectable (over 100 citations).

2. To make it very readable.

Why? Because a disproportionate number of alcoholics are not college graduates, many do not have a high school diploma. They function as alcoholism counselors because they are themselves recovering alcoholics and while most are effective, they are inclined to be suspect about any heavy, intellectualized tome about an illness they know so well. In any case, I was convinced that the book had to be interesting to read. For these reasons I included three very moving autobiographical sketches at the end of Part I, one by a published short story writer.

## Market

1. Books in Print lists dozens of texts on general counseling, *none* on counseling the alcoholic.

2. Many states have recently *upgraded certification requirements for alcoholism counselors.*

In Massachusetts this new upgrading took effect May, 1984. Included in these new requirements is didactic work. Heretofore the requirements involved only supervised, counseling practica. State colleges and extension services in Massachusetts are planning programs right now. We are here at Westfield State College. In short, I see a real boom developing for the training of alcoholism counselors in the United States. This would be an *ideal text* for such programs.

Joseph F. Perez

# ACKNOWLEDGEMENTS

A book like this could not have been written without the help of others. I am pleased to acknowledge the help of Kevin Gustafson who typed some of the counselor contributions of Part II. I am grateful for the articulate contributions of alcoholism counselors H. Richard Doerr, Mary Dumas, Judy Harrington, and Jim Kelly. I feel especially indebted to Mike McCartney, Rosemary Coombs, and Stacy Page for their candid and moving autobiographical sketches.

After me, the person who spent the most clock hours on this effort is Frances Curran. She not only typed it, but did some important editing too. I owe Fran a lot and even more to Marilyn MacKusick who provided invaluable clerical assistance and support when I sorely needed both.

Finally, and most importantly, I should like to acknowledge the help of my son, Christopher, who is an alcoholism counselor. The idea for the book came out of discussions with him. But Christopher did more than help generate the idea for it. He provided me with important research studies and enlisted and coordinated the contributions of colleagues. Without him the writing process and the ultimate completion of the book would have been most difficult.

J. F. P.

# COUNSELING THE ALCOHOLIC CONTENTS

# LIST OF FIGURES

# Part I

# THE ALCOHOLIC

## Essential Characteristics for Understanding

PART **I**

# THE ALCOHOLIC
# Essential Characteristics for Understanding

There are as many different personalities among alcoholics as there are alcoholics. At the same time certain commonalities seem to plague the personalities of those individuals suffering from the alcoholism disease. Part I will address these commonalities.

## A TRADITIONAL VIEW

### Perception

Perception is a cornerstone of human personality. How we perceive others will determine how we interact with them. If others generally are perceived as accepting when they are so, our interpersonal relations and our emotional health will be enhanced. Conversely, if we generally perceive others as threatening when they are not our own health will ultimately be demeaned. In short, how accurately we perceive the world will determine how effectively we deal with it. The judgements upon which the healthy adult acts are premised upon a mature and healthy perception of the world.

The alcoholic by definition is not healthy. Too often he/she unrealistically perceives a world filled with threat or at best indifference. Such a perception leaves the alcoholic unattuned to others and his/her sense of being devalued. Not uncommonly, judgemental responses by the alcoholic are overresponses manifested by impulsivity, escape into fantasy, and excessive personal gratification.

**Conscience**

The person without a conscience is one who engages in antisocial behavior and feels no guilt. This person is usually unable to trust or even to love. Such a person has been termed a psychopath. Most alcoholics, in their sober moments anyway, are not psychopaths. At the same time many alcoholics, drunk or sober, suffer from a conscience which fluctuates from overly scrupulous to nonexistent. Thus, when in the overly scrupulous phase the alcoholic conscience will take over the ego's judgemental functions and will make decisions out of guilt. Invariably these are self-defeating, foolish, and socially inappropriate. In the latter phase, the alcoholic may behave as if he/she were an actual psychopath demeaning, abusing and beating on those whom they ordinarily love.

The alcoholic learns early that escape into booze can effectively drown conscience at least for a little while. Unfortunately when sober, conscience returns and in even more awesome size. It is precisely to escape this awesomeness that so many alcoholics keep returning to their booze and why too, so many choose to live in their nebulous, alcoholic haze.

**Defenses**

Defenses are an innate and necessary aspect of the human personality. They feed the ego and protect it from perceived threat.

It is via defenses that healthy people are able to perceive selectively. Defenses help human beings to perceive what they want to perceive and to ignore what they want to ignore. They help to create situations, events, and interactions which are satisfying, rewarding, and at times enhancing.

With alcoholics this whole and very human process of defense becomes diseased. Their perception becomes not so much selective as distorted. And so situations, events, and interactions tend to be unsatisfying, often even demeaning.

Alcoholics, especially in the initial stages of recovery have fragile defenses. In counseling, this is usually reflected in their unsureness, in their conflicting statements. A major task of the counselor is to help these individuals to rebuild and reinforce a defense structure which helps them to perceive more realistically so that they will deal more effectively with the major problems with which they are beset. Principal among these are guilt, remorse, failure, and loss. Thus, the same defenses which were once self-defeating, which kept the alcoholics in the throes of despair now have to be redirected, restructured to help them sustain their sobriety.

Explanation and illustrations on how to redirect and restructure alcoholic defenses are provided in Part IV.

Only those defenses most commonly used by the alcoholic will be considered. These are the following:

Denial
Displacement
Fantasy
Projection
Rationalization
Reaction Formation
Regression
Repression

**Denial.** A definition for denial is the emotional refusal to acknowledge a person, situation, condition, or event the way it is. The alcoholic who consumes a fifth of scotch per day, every day, for a time may honestly not recognize any addiction to alcohol. Denial prevents any recognition of the fact.

**Displacement.** The ventilation of hostility on a person or object neither of which engendered it in the first place is displacement. To illustrate, the person under the influence or even sober who beats a spouse because he/she was hounded all day by a supervisor.

**Fantasy.** Daydreaming and a constant recourse for the alcoholic is fantasy. It is a solace especially when the alcohol is first taking effect. It is the time when the alcoholic becomes expansive, talks too loudly, boasts, etc. Fantasy may take another form for the solitary drinker. It may be the nirvana to which the alcoholic retreats to escape boredom, frustration, and anxiety. In the world of fantasy the alcoholic fulfills wishes, realizes expectations, achieves power. For many addicts, alcohol becomes the catalyst which precipitates and facilitates the creation of a synthetic reality, one far more rewarding than the real world and one to which the alcoholic feels compelled to return to again and again.

**Projection.** Motives which one harbors in oneself when attributing to another person or persons is referred to as projection. It invariably develops when a person becomes distanced from others. Estrangement and lack of communication, both the plague of the alcoholic, breed and feed this defense. Suspicion and an unhealthy like sensitivity to others manifested by a too quick to take offense attitude are common manifestations of projection. To illustrate, the alcoholic who while sipping a fourth drink becomes abusive toward a couple of strangers who are perceived to be talking about him.

**Rationalization.** This may be defined as making up excuses for actual or felt inadequacies or behaviors. This defense often is used to support denial. For example, the alcoholic who denies addiction and explains the routine need for three martinis before dinner as a way of relaxing.

**Reaction Formation.** This will be treated under Rorschach test findings.

**Regression.** Use the term regression when referring to immature behavior; to behavior which is more appropriate to an earlier chronological age. Often the behavior is intended to manipulate and/or control. Temper tantrums, sulking, and pouting are all common forms of regression in the alcoholic.

**Repression.** The term repression refers to the ego function of letting the memory of a person, situation, or event become unconscious because of fear and threat imposed by remembering it. Many individuals become repressed through the simple process of socialization. Some repression probably occurs whenever an individual is intimidated into doing and behaving in ways which are threatening or intimidating. Tahka (1966) found that alcoholics are more heavily repressed than people drawn from the normative population. Heavily repressed people are generally more unsure of themselves than lowly repressed. As developing children and adolescents they saw threat and conflict everywhere. They learned to move in it without remembering any of it. If a teacher was especially scary they repressed her as quickly as they could after leaving her. The effect of all this attitude of course is to diminish one's life experience and to reduce one's sense of sureness and one's level of maturity.

## Research Findings

Considerable testing has been done to assess the quality and strength of the alcoholic personality. The results indicate that the alcoholic functions with a weak one. One indication of this weakness is reflected in his/her impulsivity, another in his/her low tolerance for frustration. Indications are clear that heavy drinkers are far more likely to show impulsivity than are alcohol abstainers (Cisin & Cahalan, 1968). Another study came up with comparable findings. It seems that alcoholics in general have a greater tendency to act on momentary impulse than nondrinkers (Williams, 1965) and their tolerance for frustration is significantly lower than people drawn from the normal population (Cowan, Auld, & Begin, 1974).

The ability to perceive time accurately, patiently, and to respond to it appropriately also are important personality functions. There is much evidence to indicate that alcoholics are quite unable to perceive and appreciate the nature of time. Two separate studies (Roos & Albers, 1965; Sattler & Pflugrath, 1970) found that the alcoholic's perception of time is quite unlike that of the normal. Briefly, these two studies showed that the alcoholic's needs are focused upon short-term gratification. Put simply, alcoholics want what they want, when they want it—now. Two other studies confirmed these findings (Imber, Miller, Faillace, & Liberman, 1971; Smart, 1968). All of this research on the alcoholic's reaction to time discovered that alcoholics in general are quite unable emotionally to appreciate the effects of *now* behavior in their futures.

A healthy person is one who builds and maintains rewarding relationships. The alcoholic does not (Chodorkoff, 1964). Too often friends of the alcoholic are "drinking Buddies or Betties," superficial acquaintances. Relationships are founded and maintained upon ingesting alcohol with these people. This seems to be true for both men and women.

Alcoholics get divorced at a rate higher than the national average. A probable reason for this might be the fact that alcoholics have difficulty identifying with their own sexuality. They are not emotionally convinced or happy with the sex they are. Machover, Puzzo, Machover, and Plumeau (1959) using their own Figure-Drawing Test compared a group of remitted and unremitted alcoholics with a group of homosexuals and controls. The alcoholics indicated more confusion about their sexuality than did the control group. Machover et al. (1959) administered the MMPI and the Rorschach also. On these two tests the alcoholic group termed remitted revealed more signs of unconscious conflicts and anxiety about their sexuality than did the control group.

Machover's et al. (1959) findings seemed to be corroborated on a photo-preference test done by two researchers who found that male alcoholics tended to favor the pictures of older people, especially those of women. This finding was interpreted as an indication of the alcoholic's discomfort with being a man and as a response to his dependency need.

One of the most revealing studies in this area of sexual identity of the alcoholic was done by Parker (1959). He used the Terman-Miles masculinity-femininity scale and compared two groups, one confirmed alcoholics, the other, moderate drinkers. What he found was that alcoholics by and large ranked significantly lower in masculine disposition than did the moderate drinkers. The alcoholics also displayed a strong maternal dependence and had been divorced. Interestingly too, these alcoholics had come from broken homes.

In a subsequent study Parker tested a group of prealcoholics. His hypotheses were that these individuals would display a strong macho veneer and would be binding much unconscious anxiety about their sexuality. His hypotheses were confirmed (Parker, 1969). These last findings by Parker were substantiated in a subsequent study in which a group of alcoholics was tested on a different scale of conscious masculinity (Zucker, 1968).

How a person projects self to others is a product of self-understanding. The indications are clear that alcoholics by and large have a low self-concept and are hypercritical of themselves. The statistical evidence is pretty strong that alcoholics don't like themselves (Connor, 1962; Craddick & Leipold, 1968).

Finally on this same topic of self-concept, a group of 140 men were tested with the Tennessee Self-Concept Scale and compared to a sample drawn from the normal population. On all ten aspects of the scale researchers found that the alcoholics scored lower than men in general (Gross & Alder, 1970).

## WHAT PERSONALITY TESTS SHOW

Ongoing research with personality tests indicates that the alcoholic harbors a constellation of personality factors which set him/her apart from the nonalcoholic.

### Objective Personality Tests

**Minnesota Multiphasic Personality Inventory (MMPI).** One of the most widely used tests to assess personality continues to be the Minnesota Multiphasic Personality Inventory (MMPI). This test has nine different scales. The scale which has consistently reported significant difference between the alcoholic and the normal is lettered *Pd* and is concerned with measuring factors dealing with psychopathy (Button, 1956; Fuller, Lunney, & Naylor, 1966; Goss & Morosko, 1969; Hewitt, 1943; Kristianson, 1970; Spiegel, Hadley, & Hadley, 1970).The prime ingredient of psychopathy has to do primarily with a conscience which functions poorly, erratically, or not at all. In the alcoholic sometimes it takes over the personality. The alcoholic often seeks relations with other people, behaves expansively, generously, lovingly. Sometimes conscience seems to be totally absent. The alcoholic however may become a loner, disappear, embittered, convinced that no one cares a whit about him/her, because everyone is really out for self. These last feelings are related to the second prime aspect of psychopathy. Namely, an excessive concern for one's own self. The alcoholic, when in the phase of *conscience* *diminuition* tends to view the world as a hostile, threatening world where people are unnurturant, uncaring, or even out to do him/her in. When in this phase, the alcoholic is beset by constant depression frequently associated with hostility.

The MMPI test confirms this (Hoffman, 1970; Kristianson, 1970; Spiegel et al., 1970). Alcoholics generally are more depressed than most normals. What this means is that alcoholics tend to resist developing goals, to resist solution of problems in their personal lives. They resist help and may vent their anger on those closest to them. This depression in alcoholics is understandable. They are tired. They are tired of the constant emotional conflict between an overpowering and a virtually nonexistent conscience. And they are especially tired of the excessive load of guilt which they must bear when that same conscience is functioning too strongly.

**The Cattell Test—Sixteen Personality.** Cattell (Cattell, Eber, & Tatsuoka, 1970) has developed a scale (*Sixteen Factor Personality Questionnaire*) which reveals even more light on the alcoholic personality. Using his test, two researchers found a strong element of immaturity in the chronic drinker's personality (DePalma & Clayton, 1958). Alcoholics are governed by a latent but constant motive to pursue pleasure and/or to avoid any physical or psychological pain. Alcoholics, especially during adolescent and college years, appear to be constantly looking for fun and especially are not inhibited by the possible consequences of their acts. Indeed they don't even think about consequences. This focus is upon gratification—*now.*

**Jackson Personality Research Form (PRF).** Hoffman (1970b) using the *Jackson Personality Research Form* found that alcoholics score higher than normals in their need for affiliation, nurturance, succorance, and abasement. What this finding indicates is that alcoholics need people but are uncertain about how to get close to them because alcoholics don't feel that they are worthy enough to deal effectively with other people or to receive or accept the affection of others. Alcoholics in his study also scored low on aggression, autonomy, and dominance. These findings can be interpreted to mean that alcoholics also are likely to incorporate a strong element of passive dependency in their personality. This interpretation seems to be supported by low scores on achievement, play, endurance, and their high score on harm avoidance. Simply, alcoholics do not appear to be ambitious, particularly active, or interested in new experiences. Their general penchant seems to be toward a safe, warm womb-like environment.

## Projective Tests

**Rorschach Test.** This author scored and interpreted Rorschach protocols of 44 alcoholics ranging in age from 24 to 46 years. Thirty were men, 14 were women. All were middle class, employed, and paying clients in this counselor's private practice. The sample, even though select, revealed certain common denominators in personality. Thus all exhibited

—a very rich fantasy life,

—a moderate to strong need to achieve and to be respected,

—an introverted orientation,

—a moderate to high expectation of rejection,

—a prime defense of reaction formation, and

—a weak self-esteem.

What the author concluded is that alcoholics live a disproportionate part of their lives in a fantasy world. They are daydreamers who not uncommonly are beset with superstitions. Their need to succeed is strong as is their need for adulation. At the same time they are bedeviled by a latent but constant feeling that they are doomed losers. They are obsessed about this feeling and, even when they are able to put this kind of "stinkin' thinkin'" out of their cognitive minds, it remains a core part of their emotional self-understanding. It is a major reason for their fixated preoccupation with self.

Among the debilitating aspects of alcoholics' characteristics is their fearful and constant expectation of rejection. Indeed, what this counselor has learned in dealing with alcoholics is that the latter always seem to be surprised when people are accepting, a little shocked when they do for them. This perception of a rejecting world leads to problems. Frequently they take offense too quickly and worse, do it secretly, obsess about it, and may show displeasure much later to the bewilderment of the supposed offender, thereby weakening or even destroying another relationship.

Such erratic behavior may puzzle those who interact with alcoholics but it is perfectly understandable to the therapist. This behavior is a product of the psychological defense called *reaction formation.* When they use this defense, alcoholics are trying to protect themselves from perceived threat by behaving in a way which is diametrically opposed to how they really feel. Too often this is a major defense in the alcoholics' repertoire of protection. This author is convinced that reaction formation is a major debilitator of alcoholic personalities. Why? Because *it alienates alcoholics from their individual selves.* When they respond via reaction formation alcoholics do not know how they truly feel. They can't because reaction formation like all psychological defenses is unconscious.

A most insidious function of reaction formation is that it effects and maintains a low self-esteem. The importance of self-esteem cannot be overstated. It is at the very heart of all human functioning. An individual's life performance is basically a function of self-esteem. If one thinks one is good, one performs well. If one thinks one is unworthy, one performs unworthily—or one doesn't perform at all.

During the counseling process the counselor learns quickly that the alcoholic's self-esteem is low. The counselor who remains constantly aware of the alcoholic's low self-esteem can better appreciate the client's periodic embitterment, excessive concern for self, and pessimistic perception of the world to which he/she jealously adheres. The counselor can better understand also that his/her client's focus on gratification is nothing more than a puerile-like attempt to feed a badly impoverished self-esteem. Hoffman's (1970b) findings with the Jackson Personality Research Form explained previously also can be understood in this light.

**Thematic Apperception Test (T.A.T.).** The author compared the T.A.T.'s of 21 men alcoholics who were residents in a rehabilitation center with a group of nonalcoholic men who were hospitalized for physical disabilities. The alcoholics' tests were strikingly different from those of nonalcoholics. Thus the latter told mostly stories with optimistic outcomes, and focused on themes of success and effective coping strategies. The alcoholic stories, however, were characterized by themes of (1) impotence, (2) inebriation, (3) dominance, and (4) hostility. Also the author was struck by the paucity of heroes in the alcoholics' tests when compared to those of the nonalcoholics.

Vanneman (1972) has focused on this need for power in the male alcoholic. Alcoholics, these researchers have discovered, drink to accentuate their need to dominate others and because drink makes them *feel* powerful.

Resorting to drink because of an acutely low self-esteem is not a male province alone. Women drink because of self-esteem problems too. Indeed, one researcher (Beckman, 1978) found that the woman alcoholic suffers even more than the man in this regard.

Within the family, a low self-esteem can be insidiously infectious. Found in at least one study, a woman who comes from a family with a history of alcoholism is likely to develop important self-esteem problems and is herself a probable candidate for alcoholism (Beckman, Day, Bardsley, & Seeman, 1980). The irony of drinking is, of course, that while the alcoholic drinks to raise self-esteem, the effect is precisely the opposite (Konovosky & Wilsnack, 1982).

## ALCOHOLIC PERCEPTION

Alcoholics do not perceive the world nor their internal selves in the same way that do nonalcoholics. Normal people are able to differentiate between people and their setting. Alcoholics are not. For alcoholics, people and settings blend emotionally. There is little difference for them between hospital and doctor, doctor and nurse, nurse and hospital. Each and all are the institution. This inability to differentiate between figure and ground has been explained as a major reason for the alcoholics' constant dependence. Their confused inability to effectively articulate perceptually has led them to surrender to their environment. Witkin et al. (1962) in their research substantiated these views. The research showed that the perception of alcoholics is far more distorted than that of the nonalcoholics, that indeed the alcoholic dependency as a function of distorted perception is even more acute than that of nonalcoholic psychiatric patients. These studies by Witkin et al. (1962) have been corroborated by a number of researchers (Bailey, Hustmyer, & Kristofferson, 1961; Chess, Neuringer, & Goldstein, 1971; Goldstein & Chotlos, 1965; Karp, Poster, & Goodman, 1963).

The alcoholics' view of the world seems very much in-tandem with their view of themselves. Wisotsky (1958) and then again Laird (1962) found that alcoholic men when asked to Draw-A-Person were not as likely to draw a man first as are nonalcoholics. Wisotsky (1958) found that almost 95% of normals drew themselves while only 70% of alcoholics did so. Laird's (1962) findings were not too dissimilar. Eighty-one percent of the alcoholics drew themselves first compared to 95% of the normals. It would seem that the alcoholic man does not view his body as favorably as he does the woman's. Or again it may be simply that he is threatened by women.

This last thought seems to find support in another study which found that male alcoholics when asked to Draw-A-Person consistently drew the female figure taller than the male figure (Craddick & Leipold, 1968). Quite apparently alcoholic men have problems with how they perceive and accept their bodies.

Some evidence is that the alcoholic's threshold for pain is lower than that of the normal person and that his perception of pain is more acute than that of the normal person. Petrie (1967) in some sophisticated research found that the alcoholic who touched the same shock stimulus as the nonalcoholic tended to overestimate the subsequent stimulus shock. The implications of this initial research (1960s) made for interesting speculation. Could it be that some people innately feel pain, physical and psychological, more intensely than others? Could this fact be a reason that some people drink to excess? Subsequent research indicated that the answers to both questions is "yes." This study confirmed that alcoholics are more exquisitely sensitive to pain and that alcohol has a considerable reducing effect in this sensitivity. The researchers in this study hypothesized that alcoholics may be alcoholics precisely because alcohol for the heavy drinker is simply a way of effecting a physiological sensory equilibrium (Buchsbaum & Ludwig, 1981). Their hypothesis is supported in subsequent studies where it was found that alcohol effectively reduces pain more in alcoholics than it does in normals (Barnes, 1980; Brown & Cutter, 1977; Cutter, Maloof, Kurtz, & Jones, 1976).

The need to reduce pain via alcohol may have deleterious effects. Figure 1.2 contains diseases which have been shown by medical research to be caused by or related to alcohol abuse.

A related characteristic to a low threshold for pain is hypochondriasis. Alcoholics consistently score higher in this characteristic than do normals. What the research shows is that alcoholics complain more about their bodies and their emotional problems than do people drawn from the normative population (Goss & Morosko, 1970; Hagnell & Tunving, 1972; Sargent, 1966).

## What are the diseases of alcohol abuse?

***Each of the following diseases has been shown by medical research to be caused by or related to alcohol abuse.***

### ULCERS

Peptic ulcers are crater-shaped erosions occuring in the lining of the stomach and duodenum. Alcohol is extremely irritating to the stomach, and causes an oversecretion of stomach acids and enzymes. This abnormally increased acidity causes ulcers, and prevents healing of existing ulcers. The medical complications of peptic ulcers (perforation, obstruction and hemorrhaging of the stomach) are serious emergencies. No ulcer patient should drink.

### CIRRHOSIS

The liver responds to a chemical injury, such as an overdose of alcohol, by laying down scar tissue among its cells. This is called cirrhosis. Patients may appear well in early stages of this disease, but as the liver is progressively destroyed by scarring, they suffer from weight loss, nausea, vomiting, weakness, loss of sex drive, abdominal pains, bloating and bleeding. Death results from liver failure or internal hemorrhaging. Alcohol is the leading cause of cirrhosis.

### PANCREATITIS

The pancreas is a small organ lying in the uppermost portion of the abdomen, stretching from the duodenum on the right to the spleen on the left. The pancreas produces insulin and digestive enzymes, and is vital to life. Inflammation of the pancreas (pancreatitis) is a serious illness characterized by severe abdominal pains, nausea and vomiting. Alcohol is directly poisonous to the pancreas, and 40% of all pancreatitis patients are alcoholics.

### BRAIN DAMAGE

Excessive use of alcohol causes a progressive loss of brain function. This is caused by the poisonous action of alcohol on the brain together with nutritional deficiencies found in alcoholism. Studies indicate that even one single episode of deep intoxication causes some irreversible brain damage. Autopsy examinations of brains from alcoholic persons, frequently reveal a diseased condition called "wet brain", in which the normal appearance of the brain is altered.

### PNEUMONIA

The lifestyle of alcoholic persons, combined with the medical complications of alcoholism, greatly reduces resistance to infections. An illness referred to as "lobar pneumonia of drunkards" may result. The term lobar indicates that the entire lobe or division of the lung is infected. Onset of illness is usually sudden, with a shaking chill, sharp pains in the chest, cough with rusty-colored stutum, fever and shortness of breath. Delirium may accompany alcoholic pneumonia.

### DELIRIUM TREMENS

Withdrawal from alcohol, known as delirium tremens, can cause physical and emotional suffering worse than withdrawal from heroin. The DT's begin with tremors, sweating and nausea. They progress to insomnia, profound depression, delusions, confusions, hallucinations and sometimes convulsions. Unless good medical treatment is given, delirium tremens may be fatal approximately 10% of the time.

### ACCIDENTS

According to insurance statistics, alcohol is a contributing factor in 20% of falls, 20% of accidental asphyxiations, 20% of drownings, 20% of deaths from freezing, 25% of deaths attributed to choking on foods and 50% of all fatal automobile accidents. These statistics probably underestimate the roll of alcohol, but they do make their point. Accidents are far more likely to occur when alcohol is involved.

### IMPOTENCY

The belief that alcohol is an aphrodisiac or sex stimulant is pure nonsense. Alcohol is actually one of the most frequent causes of impotency. Impotency refers to the inability of a man to sustain an erection satisfactory for normal intercourse. Impotency may occur in acute alcoholism because of the depressant effect of alcohol. In chronic alcoholism it may be caused by neuritis, liver damage, malnutrition and other complications.

### MALNUTRITION

Malnutrition frequently is found in middle-stage alcoholism and is almost always present in chronic alcoholism. Deficiencies in vitamins, minerals and proteins occur because alcohol is high in calories and satisfies hunger. It is almost completely void of food value. The alcoholic person drinks, but doesn't eat. Malnutrition makes alcoholics unusually susceptible to infections, liver disease, brain damage, and many other serious abnormalities.

### CONVULSIONS

Epilepsy affects about 1 out of 200 persons and occurs slightly more frequently in males than females. Alcohol may be a direct precipitator of seizures in epileptics. Seizures may also occur in certain non-epileptic alcoholics because of the toxic effect of alcohol on the brain. A typical seizure is characterized by an outcry, loss of consciousness, falling and alternating movements of the muscles of the body. The attack usually lasts 2 to 5 minutes, and may be followed by deep sleep, headache or muscle soreness.

### CANCER OF THE ESOPHAGUS

Difficulty swallowing foods because of a sensation of blockage somewhere behind the sternum is usually the first sign of cancer of the esophagus. Diagnosis is confirmed by X-ray. Surgery is the only treatment and the cure rate is low. Because of an unknown chemical quality in alcoholic beverages, alcoholics have a far greater chance of developing cancer of the esophagus than non-alcoholics.

### ALCOHOLIC NEURITIS

Alcoholic neuritis is a condition caused by the direct poisonous effect of alcohol on the nerves of the body, as well as by certain vitamin deficiencies seen in alcoholism. Neuritis patients complain of tingling, pins-and-needles sensations, burning, itching and numbness. Weakness and paralysis follow in the late stages of neuritis. Treatment involves complete abstinence from alcohol, improved nutrition and vitamin supplementation.

### VARICOSE VEINS OF THE ESOPHAGUS

The esophagus is the food tube leading from the throat to the stomach, and its blood supply is channeled through the liver. Alcoholic persons suffering from cirrhosis of the liver develop an increase in blood pressure in the veins of the esophagus because of their liver disease. This increased pressure causes the veins to become stretched and dilated (varicose). Death from internal hemorrahaging may occur if these thin, ballooned-out veins rupture.

Figure 1.2 Diseases caused by or related to alcohol abuse.
**Note.** Reprinted by permission from *Personal Guide to Alcohol Abuse*, Spenco Medical Corporation, Waco, Texas.

# PREALCOHOLIC PERSONALITY

It is not yet certain whether or not a prealcoholic personality actually exists. The reason for this uncertainty is that there has not yet been any research which assessed potential alcoholics and reassessed them after they have become alcoholic.

There is however considerable research which suggests that alcoholics in their prealcoholic phase may differ from normals in selected personality traits. One study compared selected personality characteristics of individuals who had become alcoholic after college with nonalcoholics. Both groups had taken the tests while college freshmen. What the researchers found was that the alcoholics while freshmen were more lackadaisical and unfocused. They also were inclined to manipulate and "cut corners" without too much worry. In addition, researchers found that alcoholics tended toward a high level of unproductive activity (Loper, Kammeier, & Hoffman, 1973). These findings gibe in part with an earlier study which found that men sampled tended to be rebellious, impulsive, and nonconforming. A third study on this topic compared the test profiles of alcoholics who had been patients in a mental health clinic. They compared these files with those of a control group and found the incidence of hostility and nonconforming behavior much higher among the alcoholic group (Robins, Bates, & O'Neal, 1982). What these three studies indicated in a pretty clear fashion is that there is at least one common denominator in the individual who later becomes alcoholic and that is an inability to exercise controls effectively over the hostile impulses.

Research has been done to determine if there were factors in the alcoholic's home environment which were conducive to the development of alcoholism. What was found was that alcoholics develop poor self-esteems as children. The alcoholics in this sample were seldom reared by affectionate mothers, were exposed to much parental ambivalence, and ambiguous communication. As a child the alcoholic rarely had a clear understanding of what was expected of him/her by the adults in control of the environment. The budding self-esteem became stunted. The coordinator of this work speculated that the later addiction to alcohol was a function of this stunted self-esteem (McCord, 1972).

A study with undergraduates found that the college problem drinker already has a poor self-concept and it is comparable to that of the older alcoholic. The problem drinker in this study displayed a high incidence of self-depreciation, a low self-acceptance, and a remarkable distancing between real-self and ideal-self (Williams, 1965). The question to ask is, are these self-views a function of their already heavy drinking or are they innate predispositions? The answer is as yet unclear. More longitudinal research needs to be done to confirm the existence of a prealcoholic personality.

## ALCOHOLIC FAMILY

If the alcoholic lives with family then the addiction is a familial problem not just a personal one. When an individual begins to drink to excess, effects are felt by all members of the family. Alcoholism sickens not only the addict but the entire family. As has been indicated, the emotional deprivation suffered as a child within the family is an important factor in the development of one's alcoholism. And this seems to be truer for women than for men (Beckman, Day, Bardsley, & Seeman, 1980). One study found that when both parents are alcoholic, their children are more likely to be the same than when only one of the parents is alcoholic. This same study found that there is a higher probability for an individual to become alcoholic if one parent were so than if neither were. Quite apparently children can identify with the worst as well as the best of the parental personality.

Families have emotional equilibriums just as individuals do. Such an equilibrium has been termed a "homeostatic balance" (Jackson, 1957). This balance is achieved by how the family members perceive one another, what they expect from one another, and by how they interact with one another. Each member has a role, each plays a part in maintaining the equilibrium of the family. For example, the wife who always drives home from a party because of her husband's inebriation, the adolescent who has learned to do the family's food shopping because mother isn't feeling well—again, the husband who serves as a scapegoat for his alcoholic wife's verbal abuse. Each member consciously or unconsciously has an emotional stake in maintaining the familial equilibrium. What the author has learned is that when a member no longer wants to play the role, a change is effected within the family. The adolescent may rebel and refuse to do the family shopping, may refuse to accept mother's protestations about not feeling well and may finally confront mother and father too, about her addiction. The crisis may effect a change to which members must adapt or the family separates. The author remembers just such a case. The client, a successful architect, married for twenty-one years, was convinced by the head of his firm to join Alcoholics Anonymous. He stopped drinking and referred himself to the author for counseling. The presenting problem was not his long term drinking but a bad marriage. The wife was asked to join the counseling sessions but steadfastly refused. The client was in counseling for thirteen months and concurrently attended A.A. faithfully. What came out in the counseling was that the client, who had always had a penchant for passivity and dependence, had married a controlling, protective mother figure. She had reinforced his dependency by tolerating his drinking but had kept the knowledge secret from their children and their friends. She even bought his booze. In a real sense she had fed his alcoholism. When his drinking stopped, his need for a protective mother figure also stopped and the family equilibrium changed. She could not adapt. Simply, she functioned better with an alcoholic husband than with a sober husband. She filed for divorce.

There is research which shows that the self-esteem of married couples drops as their consumption of alcohol increases. There is little doubt that an alcoholic man can wreak emotional havoc in the family setting. There is research evidence which shows, however, that the effects of a woman's alcoholism are even worse. Curlee (1970) compared male and female patients at an alcoholic treatment center and found that once a woman took to drink her problems became more acute more rapidly than they did for a man. A reason for this may be found in the results of another study which found that female alcoholics have lower self-esteems than do male alcoholics (Beckman, 1978).

Apparently effects of female alcoholism on family members can be severe. Indeed, two researchers found that students' reasons for drinking were positively related to the frequency of maternal intoxication. The researchers went on to say that a male or female student's risk of becoming a problem drinker increased if he/she had been exposed to what the authors of the study called "maternal deviant, drinking." Quite apparently, the negative impact of an alcoholic mother is greater than that of an alcoholic father. This fact is probably because the maternal alcoholism is less socially acceptable than is paternal alcoholism.

# ALCOHOLIC ADOLESCENTS

Drinking among adolescents today is rampant. The National Institute on Alcohol Abuse estimates that thirty percent of all adolescents who drink have little or no control over it. This inability to control drinking is the reason that more than ten thousand adolescents are traffic fatalities every year (Hawthorne & Menzel, 1983).

One estimate places the number of alcoholic adolescents at ten percent of the adolescent population (comparable with the adult drinking population). If these estimates are accurate, this would mean that today approximately six hundred thousand adolescents have a serious drinking problem (Keller, 1980).

Even more alarming than these statistics is a report that a "very substantial evidence of alcohol use exists throughout the drug treatment population" (Hubbard, Cavanaugh, Rachal, Schlenger, & Ginzburg, 1983) and that the programs designed to treat adolescent alcoholism have not had the positive effect expected. Thus over a third of the adolescents treated in programs funded by the National Institute on Alcohol Use continue to use alcohol in excessive amounts (Hubbard et al., 1983).

The evidence is that adolescents (both boys and girls) take their first drink during age thirteen. This fact has been true for over twenty years. What has not been true for over twenty years, however, is that adolescent boys report their first experience of being drunk as occurring at age thirteen (Fromme & Samson, 1983). In short, the intensity of the addiction as well as the generality among adolescents seems to have become more acute.

For a long time now adolescents have viewed drinking as an important complementary rite to facilitate passage into adulthood. Drinking in their view was and is the "cool thing" to do (Rachal, Guess, Hubbard, Maisto, Cavanaugh, Waddell, & Benrud, 1983). "Has to be," they reason, "all the adults do it." Thus, when still a child the adolescent observed that men drink. Women drink. Dad drinks. Mom drinks. "So why shouldn't I drink?" becomes the logical next question. And each does.

We shouldn't be surprised nor especially alarmed at that fact. What is alarming is that a disproportionate number of adolescents are growing up without experiencing the adolescent years. They relate to parents, teachers, and peers through an alcoholic haze and so are unable to acquire the social and interpersonal skills historically acquired during adolescence. The alcoholic "buzz" does not permit them to. Via this buzz they are able to escape any and all potential anxiety, pain, frustration, and ambiguity (Milman, Bennett, & Hanson, 1983).

In short they emerge from the teen years with the social sophistication and emotional wherewithal of children. *And they know it.* It is probably for this reason that the male adolescent problem drinker continues to be a problem drinker in his twenties. The negative effects of alcoholic addiction during the adolescent years are not all emotional or social. There is evidence that there are others. For example, Hannon, Day, Butler, Larson, and Casey (1983) found that there is a decline in intellectual competence with constant alcoholic addiction.

Many of those who study the alcoholic adolescent point to the peer group as the critical cause for adolescent's addiction. Thus, they will cite studies which show that a given adolescent's drinking increases as peers increase their drinking (Harford & Spiegler, 1982). They report that excessive drinking during the early college years is a function of peer pressure (Shore, Rivers, & Berman, 1983).

There is little doubt that peer groups are an important factor in the development of adolescent alcoholism. This author however believes that the family can obviate destructive peer group influence. A peer group assumes major importance in an adolescent's life precisely when the family is not meeting his/her basic needs of security, love, and self-esteem. Generally speaking, when a family has been successful in meeting those needs during the childhood years, drinking during adolescence is not a problem. The notable exception to this generalization, of course, is when one or both of the parents are alcoholic (McKenna & Pickens, 1981).

What most adults forget, too easily, is that adolescents are still in the formative learning years and at some level still want guidance. If home was always the place that the adolescent received solid, valid, enhancing modeling, and information he/she will as an adolescent continue to seek modeling first there. This is particularly true about drinking. There is research evidence, for example, which suggests that an adolescent's drinking behavior is very much a function of parental approval and disapproval. Adolescents reported that they drank little if their parents disapproved, much if their parents approved (Rachal et al., 1983). That the home has a moderating effect on drinking is reflected in a recent study which shows that adolescents sharply reduce alcoholic consumption in the home but increased it in the peer settings (Harford & Spiegler, 1983).

## Case of Linda R

This case exemplifies the insidious, destructive hold that alcoholic parents can have upon their children. The author dealt with Linda while a consultant in a school department. The reports which follow are the actual ones. The minor editing and name changes were done to insure identity of the subject.

Linda was referred by her guidance counselor. She was reported as being out of contact in her classes. "Unreachable" was the word used most often to describe her class behavior. Linda was failing in all of her classes. She was suspected of drinking. A teacher had caught her in the girls' room nipping from a bottle of wine. Twice liquor had been smelled on her breath.

### Psychodiagnostic Report.

**Name:** Linda R

**Testing Date:** 13 Jan 1974

**Date of Birth:** 17 Sept 1960

**Tests Administered:**

Wechsler Intelligence Scale for Children,
Bender Gestalt Test,
Thematic Apperception Test, and
Rorschach

**Behavioral Observation:** Linda is a short, slender, pale faced girl who wears glasses. She showed up for testing in a skirt and blouse which were clean but wrinkled and ill fitting. Her shoes were well worn and of a vintage passe. Linda covered her mouth when she spoke or smiled to hide a missing tooth and a few badly crooked ones. Initially she was detached and shy but warmed up as the testing proceeded. Quite apparently, she enjoyed the attention she received from the testing session.

**Test Results:** Linda is currently functioning with a verbal I.Q. of 115, a performance I.Q. of 115, and a full scale I.Q. of 116. Scores such as these indicate that Linda functions in the bright-normal range of intelligence. Approximately 75% of the people in her age score *below* her on this test. Linda has the ability to obtain A's and B's.

In the verbal sphere of competency Linda functions best in general fund of information, vocabulary, and reasoning. In all of these areas, she functions like a person two years her senior. Her memory and ability to reason arithmetically are consistent with her general level of competency. She functions in the low normal ranges in social comprehension.

In the nonverbal spheres her ability is in the superior to very superior ranges in spatial relations but below average in both perception and social awareness.

The WISC findings seem to be substantiated by Rorschach findings. What we have here is a confused little girl who is growing up with glaring deficiencies in the social and interpersonal spheres. Linda is bewildered, shy, confused, and socially scared. She perceives a world filled with hostile or at best indifferent strangers. Such a perception has led to a general mistrust of acquaintances and teachers. (She reports she has no friends.)

Quite apparently this is a girl who has been emotionally shortchanged during most of her life. She is in desperate need for attention of any sort. Her failing record can be understood as a function of her self-perception. Simply stated, Linda sees herself as a failure.

**Recommendations:** Home visit to assess conditions. Counseling at earliest possible time.

Joseph F. Perez, Ph.D.
Consulting Psychologist

**Report of Social Worker.** Linda lives on the one street of this town which could be accurately described as "slummy." An only child, she lives with her parents in a duplex house which sorely needs a coat of paint and the two front steps repaired.

I visited the home without benefit of an appointment because there is no phone and Linda was always vague and unwilling about helping to arrange the visit. I learned why when I got there. Both parents were home. I never got to see the father but I heard him only too well. He snored loudly in the bedroom off the kitchen throughout the interview. Mrs. R told me that he was sleeping off a half-gallon of wine.

Mrs. R seemed oblivious to the untidy even dirty kitchen. The small living room was only a little better. Mrs. R told me she was 38 years old. She appears to be ten to fifteen years older. Her bleary look and confused speech convinced me that she too had had her share of the half gallon of wine.

The interview was a very short one because Mrs. R was uninterested and not a little embarrassed by my presence. I did learn that Mr. R is an unemployed welder who suffers from a "bad back." The family is on the city welfare rolls and has been for almost a decade.

What I saw in her house convinces me that Linda's problems are considerable. Both parents are alcoholics and oblivious to any problems Linda might have.

I concur with Dr. Perez, Linda should be in counseling. After seeing her mother and her home I am not optimistic.

M. Corcoran
School Social Worker

**Comments.** After reading this report the author arranged to see Linda on Monday mornings and Thursday afternoons. Our sessions lasted forty-five minutes. Linda was so starved for attention that despite her suspiciousness and shyness, and perhaps because of our prior testing session, rapport was almost immediate.

Toward the end of the first session and continuing for many weeks she spent the entire forty-five minutes describing the utter deprivation in which she had been reared. The author still remembers some of her lines. "I was always alone. I don't remember ever being held even... I saw the boy next door being spanked once for playing on the street. I remember going on the street to play. I guess I wanted to be spanked. My mother and father didn't even notice. They were both too drunk." Once after a particularly tearful session she confided her abiding fear—that she would end up like her parents. Despite the defeatist attitude which threaded through her talk, Linda had an engaging way about her. The utter simplicity and candor with which she related the rejection and loneliness of her life was touching. So much so that the author stepped out of his counseling role and began to try to manipulate her life outside of counseling. He arranged through a dentist friend to have dental work done, her tooth replaced, the others straightened.

He continued seeing Linda for the balance of that academic year and for all of the next. Throughout he knew she had a crush on him. He used it and began to communicate his expectations about her school work. By the end of the first year of counseling, Linda was making first honor roll, had a part-time job, and new clothes. She began dating.

The following September Linda turned sixteen and never came back to school. She had obtained a full-time job in a local factory. She called the author at Christmas time of her sixteenth year to say that she was happily married and pregnant. The guidance counselor subsequently informed the author that Linda had never married.

**Personal Note.** Once while driving I saw Linda coming out of her parents house, a baby in tow. I stopped to talk. She never met my gaze but kept glancing away with a vague, defeated look. I had seen that look before. But never in anyone so young. It was the look of the alcoholic who has surrendered to life.

## ALCOHOLISM—THE PROGRESSION

Alcoholism is a progression. In Figure 1.3 are illustrated acts occurring during alcohol addiction and recovery.

E. M. Jellinek in 1951 delivered a series of lectures entitled *The Phases of Alcohol Addiction in Males.* This series was later expanded by Glatt (1959). The description of the four progression stages toward and recovering from alcoholism is derived from their work.

The following description is intended only as a general guide. Few alcoholics actually progress step by step through the four stages as described. Indeed, there are alcoholics who may become addicted with their first drink and touch on steps of the fourth stage in a matter of months even weeks. Others might take decades to do so.

**Stage I**

1. Regular social drinking. The individual is uncomfortable when there is no booze at a party or social event.

2. Seldom leaves a party not high.

3. A gradual almost imperceptible increase in tolerance for alcohol.

4. The two "quick ones" after work and/or before dinner become a regularity.

5. Occasionally resort to alcohol under pressure.

6. Drinks more quickly and uncommonly more than others.

**Stage II**

1. Begins occasional drinking at odd times during the day.

2. Drinking under pressure increases.

3. Sneaking of drinks begins.

4. Delays eating to continue drinking.

5. Guilt feelings about drinking.

6. The onset of memory blackouts.

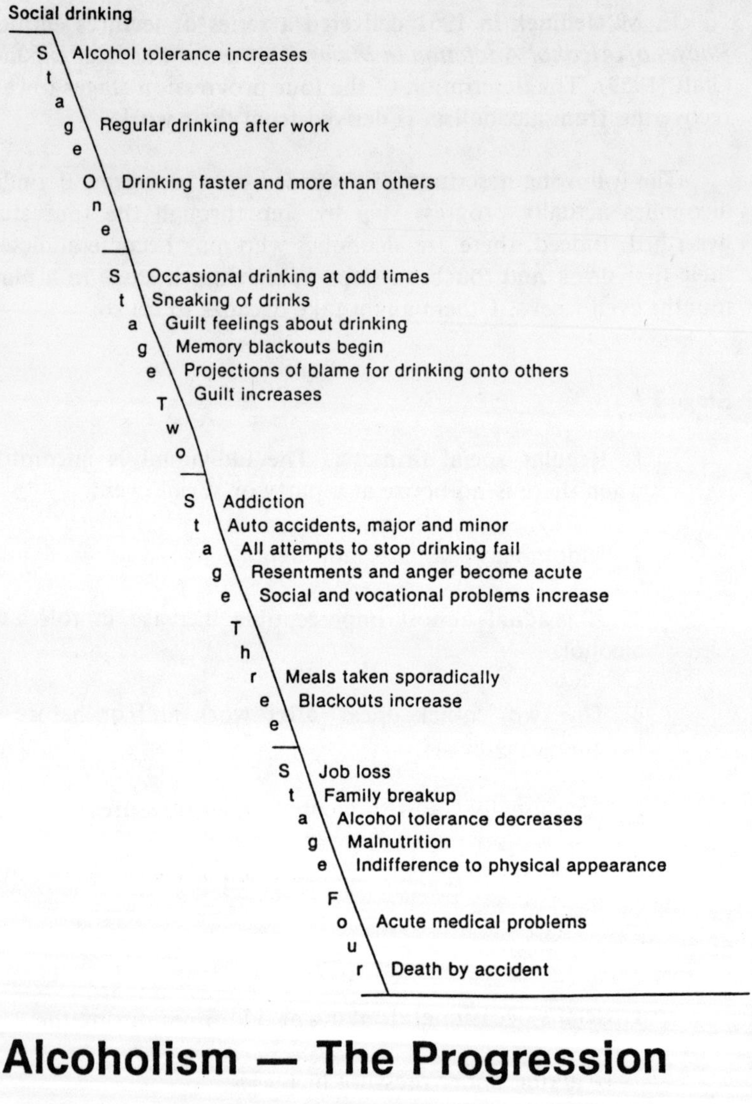


Figure 1.3 Schematic for alcoholism—progression and recovery process.

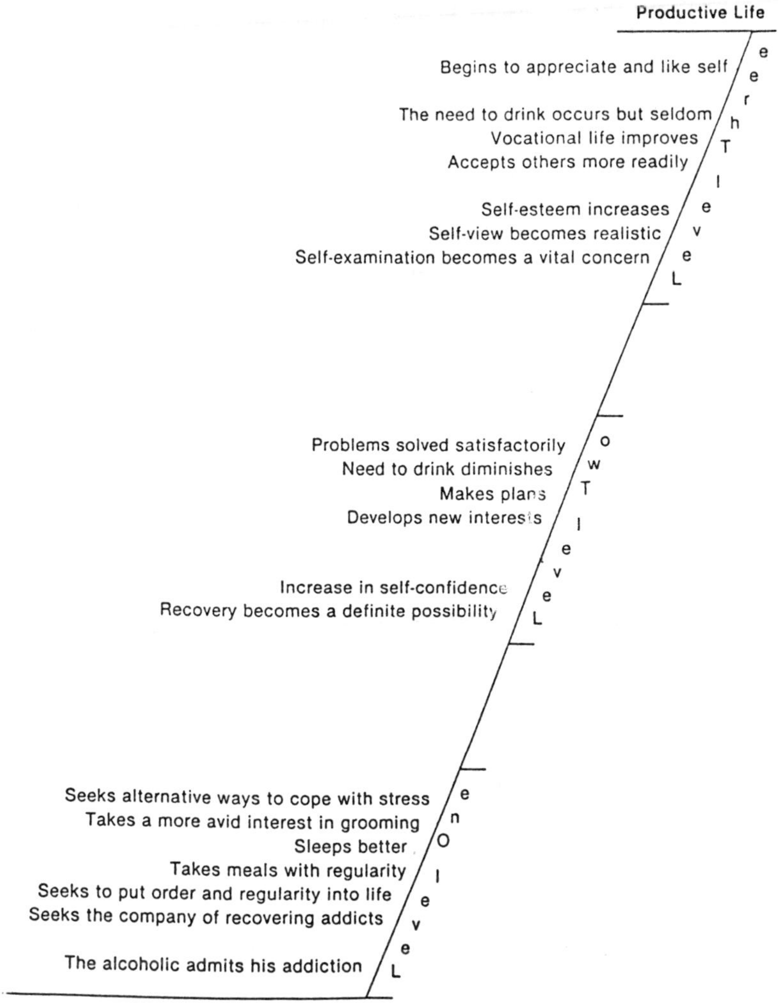


# Alcoholism — The Recovery Process

7. Begins to project blame for drinking onto persons, situations, or events.

8. Begins to find fantasy rewards in drinking.

9. Friends and family begin to notice. Reproofs and chastisements begin to occur.

10. Guilt increases. Attempts made to stop.

**Stage III**

1. Psychological addiction has occurred. Control over drinking at a very low ebb.

2. Speeding tickets and auto accidents, minor and major.

3. All attempts at stopping drinking fail.

4. Resentments, anger toward friends and family become acute.

5. Social and vocational problems increase.

6. Keeps problem hidden.

7. Meals are taken sporadically.

8. Seeks out drinking "Buddies and Betties."

9. Solitary drinking increases.

10. Blackouts increase.

**Stage IV**

1. Beset by a constant stage of anger and/or depression.

2. Job loss may occur.

3. Drinking becomes the lone interest.

4. Family break-up may occur.

5. Lives in an alcoholic daze or constant binge, drinking for days at a time.

6. Alcohol tolerance may decrease.

7. Malnutrition may set in.

8. Overnight stays at a hospital.

9. Lack of concern in grooming and physical appearance.

10. Acute medical problems appear, i.e. liver cirrhosis.

11. Death by accident.

## ALCOHOLISM—THE RECOVERY PROCESS

The first step in the recovery process levels (admission of alcoholism) is a very personal and private matter. Why it occurs or doesn't, remains a mystery. For some individuals it occurs in Stage I of the Progression outlined previously, for others not until Stage IV, and for some, never.

The following three levels for the process of recovery like that of the four stages for progression into alcoholism is intended only as a general description. This process is not an easy, neat, and simple step by step movement, level to level to level. Indeed, the return back to a meaningful life is fraught with peril, anguish, temptations by the score and not unoccasionally, despair. In short, few alcoholics make this return with ease but some do make it. The autobiographical sketches which follow the summary show that.

**Level I**

1. The alcoholic admits alcoholism.

2. Honestly asks for help.

3. Learns about addiction, is willing to see it as an illness.

4. Seeks the company of recovering addicts.

5. Begins to find reward in a chosen form of therapy, individual, group or recreational.

6. Seeks to put order and regularity into life.

7. Takes meals with regularity.

8. Sleeps better.

9. Takes a more avid interest in grooming.

10. Seeks to find ways to cope with normal stresses of living.

**Level II**

1. Recovery becomes a definite possibility.

2. Increase in self-confidence.

3. Takes a more active interest in others.

4. Develops new interests.

5. Makes plans.

6. Gets verbal rewards and encouragement from family and friends.

7. The need to drink diminishes.

8. Problem solving, obligations are dealt with, if not always perfectly at least satisfactorily.

**Level III**

1. Self-examination becomes a vital concern.
2. Self-view becomes realistic.
3. Self-esteem increases.
4. Guilt is put into proper perspective.
5. The need to drink occurs but seldom.
6. Sees recovery as a life process toward a sense of fulfillment.
7. Accepts people.
8. Vocational life improves dramatically.
9. Begins to appreciate self and own productivity.
10. A life-long process of coping with guilt with confidence.

## ALCOHOLISM—THE RELAPSE

Alcoholics who are in counseling and who have seemingly made an emotional commitment to stop drinking frequently return to the bottle. For some it is because their commitment is something less than genuine, for others it is because of the fear engendered by what they see in the self-examination process of counseling, and for still others it is because of the threat imposed by the realization that continued sobriety necessitates a radical change in self-perception, perception of others, and lifestyle in general.

The counselor should know that there is another reason that clients lapse back into drink. *They are testing the hypothesis upon which the whole process is premised; namely, that they are alcoholic.* Thus, they reason if they are drinking they aren't really alcoholic, and so don't really have to self-examine. In short, they don't really have to change. In their fuzzed way of thinking their ability to drink is proof of their normalcy, of their health.

The relapse can be short term, protracted, or the pathway to death. In every case it is a classic illustration of the denial defense.

Symptoms of the relapse frequently can be found in sudden and new client behaviors. These fall into four general categories:

1. Behavioral

2. Verbal

3. Emotional

4. Body Language

**Behavioral**

The most obvious evidence of relapse is the *odor of alcohol.* Too many counselors (especially new ones) deny that they smell or think they smell liquor on their client's breath. They like to perceive the new gum chewing, peppermint sucking habit displayed by a client as a healthy alternative to booze.

If counselors think they smell booze, they should verbalize it to their clients especially if the client is one who never chewed anything before. The counselor's verbalization may be a blunt question or an observation toned fecitiously. The style should gibe with the counselor's manner and personality. In any case, once the counselor makes the remark he/she should observe the response carefully and proceed from there.

Another possible evidence of relapse is *the client who comes in one day heavily perfumed or cologned.* The author's experience is that the client is trying to mask the odor of alcohol or is trying to redirect the counselor's perception. A remark by the counselor, pointed or subtle, is not inappropriate.

*Being unusually early or late for an appointment* is often a sign of a relapsed client. In the former situation the client may be showing an inappropriate zeal for counseling (he/she protesteth too much). At the same time the client who suddenly starts showing up unusually early may be crying out that he/she is indeed on the brink of relapse.

Clients who suddenly start coming late for their appointment communicate that their motivation for counseling is on the wane. More often than not such behavior reflects a client in or tending toward relapse.

*Continued missed appointments* because of "sickness" may well be a sign of relapse. Clients should always be asked about them. And again, their responses should be carefully observed.

*Sudden weight gain* is frequently a symptom of relapse. If the counselor one day observes that the client seems heavier, the counselor should inquire about it. In any social context, and in most other *counseling* contexts this would be considered inappropriate. In alcoholism counseling it is appropriate and a very worthy topic for discussion. Why? The simple truth is that when a client stops drinking he/she ordinarily *loses* weight or at worst maintains it even if they increase their nutritional or junk food intake.

In sum, behavior by clients which seems out of the ordinary should be confronted by the counselor. It is the counselor's obligation to let clients know that the counselor is sensitive to any and all changes which might be syptomatic of a relapse.

**Verbal**

The verbal manner of the client in relapse is different. The difference can be subtle, blatant, or somewhere in between.

Clients in relapse frequently *fudge their replies.* They suddenly seem unable to make a statement without couching it in qualifications, i.e., "Yeah, I'm going to try to do that. That just might be a good idea you got there, doc, and if I get a chance and if things are right, I might just do it."

Clients in relapse frequently *change the subject* especially if it even remotely borders on the possibility of their being in a relapse. Such clients seem to verbally flee from questions posed by the counselor, from subjects which smack of the client's attempted con of the counselor.

Clients who suddenly develop a new verbal style of launching into *long, rambling monologues* are legitimate suspects of relapse. This is a ploy used by the client who needs to control the counseling hour because of the fear of being found out.

*Discussions about former drinking associates* delivered in almost nostalgic tones should be viewed suspiciously by the counselor. At its most innocent level such talk should tell the counselor that the client has not yet learned to fill the time or social void provided by the client's prior drinking bouts.

A not uncommon verbal manisfestation of relapse is the client's sudden *request for additional appointments.* What this means often is that the client is in conflict and is crying out for help. If at all possible, such a client should be given the additional appointments and at the same time the counselor should make it transparently clear that finally it is the client's decision to drink or to abstain, that the client's ego not the counselor's is the locus of control.

**Emotional**

The client in relapse always seems more nervous. Frequently there is *a dramatic increase in the amount of tears shed* in a counseling session and not just when the client is female either.

Client *voices seems to be more strident* and far less modulated. Unaccountably client sentences seem to be inappropriately punctuated with nervous laughs, giggles, and guffaws.

**Body Language**

The client in relapse tells the counselor as much with his/her body. The sudden onset or uncommon increase in each of the following signs may be symptomatic of a relapse.

- Averting of the eyes
- Fidgeting
- Nervous twitching, hand drumming
- Slight, almost indefinable eye glaze

- Facial puffiness

- Constant, latent, unaccountable glint of fear in the eyes; a vulnerable look; scared rabbit look

- Client begins to sit at attention and seemingly listens too intently, or the vice-versa

If any of the above signs were to be manifested with one or more of the others, the counselor should be especially concerned.

A point worthy of reiteration is that the body language which communicates a relapse most clearly is that language which the counselor finds ''foreign'' and new in the client's personality.

## SUMMARY

Perception is a cornerstone of human personality. How we perceive others will determine how we interact with them. Too often the alcoholic perceives a world filled with threat or at best indifference. Not uncommonly, this is manifested by impulsivity, escape into fantasy, and excessive personal gratification.

The alcoholic conscience is characterized by fluctuation between over-scrupulousness and nonexistence. In the former phase, the alcoholic's behavior is a function of guilt. In the latter, the behavior brutalizes those near him/her.

Alcoholics' psychological defenses do not work often because they are used immoderately and because an undue quantity and intensity of threat is perceived.

Alcoholics experience difficulty in building and maintaining relationships. A probable reason for this variable is that they have trouble identifying with their own sexuality. This difficulty with self-identification is reflected in a low self-esteem, and paradoxically in an excessive concern for one's own self. This constant conflict results in depression, and when depressed the alcoholic withdraws into the safe, warm womb-like environment of addiction.

In his research with the Rorschach, the author discovered that the alcoholic has a rich fantasy life, a moderate to strong need to achieve and to be respected, an introverted orientation, a moderate to high expectation of rejection, a weak self-esteem. Reaction-formation is a prime defense.

The author's research with the T.A.T. indicated that the alcoholic is characterized by feelings of impotence, is obsessed with the need to drink, feels victimized, harbors deep hostility, and has trouble identifying with hero types.

The alcoholic's perception is that of one who has surrendered to his/her environment. The alcoholic man tends to view the woman's body as threatening and more prestigious than his own. Alcoholics perceive and anticipate pain more sensitively than do normals. Alcohol seems to have a more soothing effect upon them than upon normals. This perception and anticipation helps to explain why the alcoholic has a stronger penchant for hypochondriasis than does the normal person.

It is not yet certain whether a prealcoholic personality actually exists. However, there is some evidence that individuals who lack controls may have a higher predisposition toward alcoholism than do those with normal controls. Also, an emotionally depriving home environment may be conducive toward the development of a prealcoholic personality. However, the view by most professionals is that more longitudinal research needs to be done to confirm the existence of an alcoholic personality.

Alcoholism is not a personal but a familial problem. Maternal alcoholism seems to have a more devastating effect upon the familial homeostasis than does paternal alcoholism.

The high incidence of alcoholism among adolescents is a legitimate cause for alarm because a high percentage of them emerge from the teen years with social and interpersonal skills of children. The peer group contributes toward the destructive-like drinking but the author holds that the family can be a critically important factor for obviating or aggravating the process.

The Jellinek and Glatt curves served as the basis for the description of alcohol progression and recovery. Progression began at Stage I with social drinking and continued into the fourth stage with death as a possible outcome. The recovery process was explained as beginning with denial and continues lifelong.

Alcoholics go into relapse for a variety of reasons, and manifest their relapse in a myriad of behaviors. These behaviors fall into four general categories: (1) Behavioral, (2) Verbal, (3) Emotional, and (4) Body Language. The counselor should be suspicious of sudden, new, and inconsistent behavior by the client as it may be a sign of relapse.

## TOPICS FOR DISCUSSION

1. How does an understanding of an alcoholic's perception of the world help to better understand him/her?

2. How can an appreciation of the alcoholic conscience equip the counselor to counsel him/her more effectively?

3. How can an awareness of the alcoholic system of defense aid the counselor?

4. How are perception, defense and conscience related to building and maintaining relationships?

5. How can an appreciation of the alcoholic's fear of rejection help the counselor to function better?

6. What are the most striking differences between an alcoholic personality and a "normal" personality?

7. How can the knowledge that alcoholics perceive and anticipate pain more sensitively than do normals help the alcoholism counselor?

8. If an alcoholic has a problem, why is it more prudent to view the problem from a familial rather than an individual perspective?

9. Why are some adolescents so easily prone to peer influence and others not?

10. Which of all the symptoms discussed under relapse do you consider to be the most telling? Why?

## THREE AUTOBIOGRAPHICAL SKETCHES

In Figure 1.4 is illustrated the cycle of addiction. This cycle can be found in what alcoholics say if one listens to the stories they tell.

The author fully appreciates the fact that there is an element of arrogance in writing about the alcoholic experience when one is not himself an alcoholic. In order to mitigate that fact, the author asked three recovering alcoholics to write about their experience. These are their stories.

### Male, 41, Divorced Father, a College Teacher

*For 16 years I had lived as a hunted and haunted man, struggling each day to avoid detection and, when trapped, frantically trying to escape the truth and its consequences. On Saturday night, May 2, 1981, there was no safety left in the small apartment I shared with my girlfriend and I knew I had to flee. I was too drunk to get myself out of there, having polished off three quarts of gin in the preceding 24 hours. Still, I had to make a getaway because the hideous gnarled gnomes and glowing bugs and disconnected voices had slipped through the walls and windows and were amassing for a final assault on my alcohol-soaked body and brain. If they broke through the last thin membrane of my exhausted psychic defenses this night, I knew they might drag me forever into that living nightmare of stark-raving madness from which there seemed no escape.*

# The Cycle of Addiction

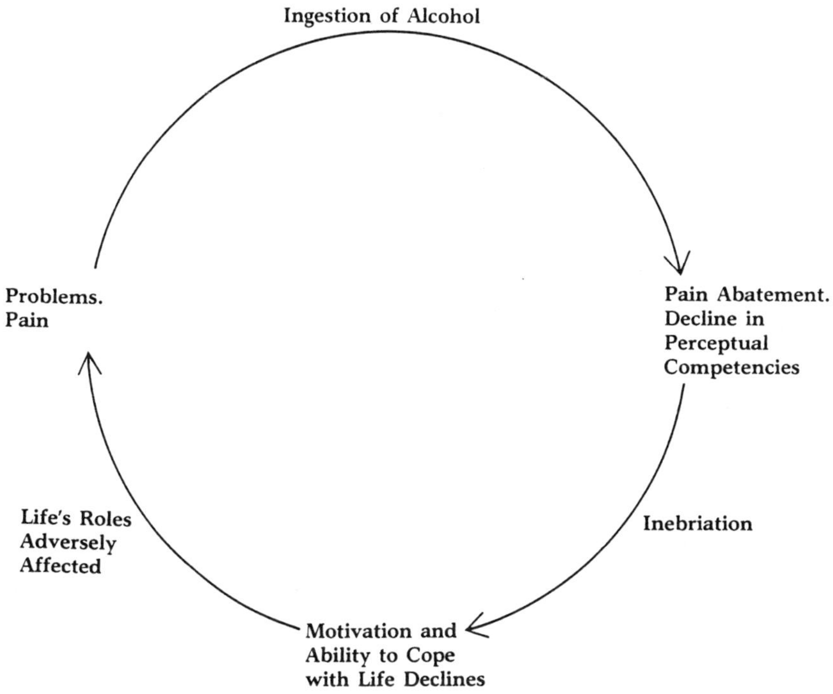


Figure 1.4 Schematic illustration of the cycle of addiction.

*I asked my girlfriend to drive me to my sister's home some fifty miles away, and when she asked me "why" I had no answer. To this day I don't know why I chose that particular place as an attempted refuge, but I was insistent. Although she saw no point in it, the urgency of my pleading and the absence of any notion as to what else to do persuaded that confused and frightened woman to oblige my request.*

*Once there, my sister, her fiance, and my girlfriend tried to fathom my condition and to make me comfortable, and then they went to bed. I wanted to sleep too. So often in the past few years all I longed for was the chance to fade into a state of numb nothingness, of painless unconsciousness and unfeeling oblivion, that would last forever.*

*But when I tried that night, sleep would not come. I was terrified to find that I had been followed by the phantoms I had sought to escape. When I closed my eyes my mind turned over and over like a whirling flywheel, flashing a kaleidoscope of images and thoughts and fears that had no relationship to each other, or for that matter to anything. I dug my fingers into my scalp to stop this insane parade inside my skull, but ugly little trolls just laughed at the vanity of my feeble effort to control something I could not touch or influence or understand. My arms and legs twitched and jumped involuntarily, as if those phantoms were jolting me sadistically with a cattle prod. I wrapped the pillow around my head, to no avail.*

*I got up and went to the living room and put on the light and spent the rest of the night pacing the carpet trying to walk around the ragged edges of panic. I knew the landscape of panic well, for I had lived with it or the threat of it, every day since a March Sunday in 1965. I was at Mass that morning when it first began as a slight tremor in my hands, a pounding in my chest, and clammy sweat on my forehead, a vague sense of anxiety, about nothing in particular. I was sick with a terrible hangover that day in church and I first attributed the symptoms to that. But then, like a tidal wave sweeping up and over me, a sense of abject terror and imminent doom produced a violent shaking, a profuse cold sweat that drenched me, a heart that seemed about to explode, a sense that my knees had vanished and left my lower legs disconnected from my thighs and a ringing alarm in my intestines. I had felt that I was literally coming apart at the seams of my skin and that my mind was escaping the confines of my body and slipping into a hellish twilight zone of horror never before visited by another human being.*

*That day I knew for the first time the incredible terror, the total unworldliness, the horrid fright of abject helplessness a person feels when the mind and soul somehow disconnect themselves from some delicate tether of flesh and blood that moors them to the mainstream of humanity, of acceptance, of rootedness, of belongingness. With alarms clanging in every fiber of my body and my mind eluding my grasp like wind-swept vapor any possibility of communication. I felt I was on the verge of losing all control over my behavior. I saw myself being wrestled down, placed in a straight-jacket, and salted away in an asylum. To prevent that, I knew I had to get a grip on myself and pull myself back from the edge of madness, but I literally rattled with fear as I realized that I did not know how. I knew hell, that day.*

*I did not know that five years of heavy daily drinking had brought me to this mental cliff. All I knew was that I wanted to draw back from the edge and never get near it again. I bolted out of the church, ran home as if pursued by devils, wrenched the cap off my gin bottle, and with the neck clanking against the lip of the glass, I poured myself a tumbler full and drank it like water. Slowly, the alcohol eased me back into the tranquility of a lazy Sunday morning. It seemed I had my answer, and from that day forward for 16 years I never allowed myself to be more than an arm's length from the toxic medicine, the deceitful distilled spirits that seemed to be the only friend I could rely on to ward off the evil spirits of insanity that lurked in wait for me everywhere.*

*Unwittingly, I had like Faust, sold my soul to the devil, in exchange for alcohol's promise to spare me from slipping away forever from the farthest reaches of any human contact or self control. To keep me from the desolate moonscape of total loneliness and depravity, I surrendered everything I ever owned of both a material and spiritual nature. I had planned to be with my father on a July night in 1972 when he called and asked me to come—I simply wanted a couple of martinis to make the trip more pleasant. I was still drinking alone, hours later, when he gave up the wait and died. The death certificate said it was a miocardial infarcation, but only I could know he was killed by a broken heart. I was drunk at his wake and at his funeral.*

*I wanted to give my little son the only thing he asked, a few hours of my time. But I needed to drink, so I said "no" to the hope in his freckled face. When his eyes dimmed and his tiny red head hung, I did not relent, but stood there torn between love and addiction as he moped away, dejectedly kicking at the stones in his path to confusion, hurt, and loss. I wanted the love of my picture-perfect daughter, a kid so inside-out beautiful that she's a blessing to the human race, but I so much needed to put alcohol first that I was able to bear hearing her make but one request of me, her brown eyes blinking back tears, "Daddy, please! Just go away and don't come back!" I knew the colitis that ate my gorgeous wife's guts out was caused by my drinking and I saw the scars of my disease mar her body and I knew she was right when she sobbed and stamped her foot and screamed, "You're murdering me!" I wanted it to be different, but what could I do? I had to drink or I would go crazy, and only I could know that, for only I had been to the brink. I would lose all before I lost my mind.*

*Then that May in 1981, as the sun rose and still I paced, I knew I could no longer move fast enough or far enough to survive. I had tried everything. I had, a few weeks before, even gone with a gun and parked on a deserted dirt road in the woods. I had put the barrel in my mouth and tasted it, a cold, blue-black, acidic, iron assurance on a fuzzy, fermented tongue that a simple twitch of my finger would bring the eternal relief from remorse, despair, and self contempt that plagued my every conscious hour. I was killing the living love of so many innocent people, why should I not do something noble, and at the same time, achieve what I now believed to be the only final answer to my pain? I was a bum, now. My family had thrown me out. I was divorced from everything tangible and intangible that I had ever belonged to or that had ever belonged to me. My girlfriend said she could no longer tolerate my behavior, and I was only headed back to the cheap flops peopled by troubled transients from which she had given me refuge. I would be back on streets that led nowhere, toting all I had left in the world in the half-filled sea bag. Soon, I would probably be totally unable to work and I would lose my job, and with it, the money I needed to pay the ransom to alcohol which held my mind hostage. Why not pull the trigger?*

*The headlights of my car reflected on a white sign nailed to a tree in those woods. I read it. It said, "No Hunting." This was what I had come to. I was going to shoot myself on a dark and moonless night in a lonely place where sane people had decreed it illegal to shoot even the wild rodents that foraged in the night to feed off of each other. Wasn't there a sign somewhere that protected me? Or had I sunk too low? Or was this the sign?*

*In a sense, it was. That had been the early part of my last drunk, a desperate, downward spiral that had led me to the home of my sister, who happened to work at a hospital that had an alcohol detoxification and rehabilitation program. "Why," she asked that Sunday morning, "don't you let us take you there? They can probably give you some tips on how to handle your drinking better." She wasn't, she promised, saying that I was an alcoholic or that I should admit myself to the hospital. She was just saying I might get some good advice. I went, not to get good advice, but in the hope that I would get some tranquilizers, for hospitals and doctors had always come to my rescue with pills.*

*But this ward of this hospital was different. It was staffed by alcoholics and people especially trained in the symptoms and treatment of alcoholism. They said I should stay there for 21 days and I protested. What would my friends think? The answer was that any friends who did not know I belonged there were not the kinds of friends I needed. What about my job? The answer was that my job could and would wait. But what about my life? If I stay, I'll be admitting that I'm an alcoholic and won't that mess up my whole life? The answer was raucous laughter. My hands shook so badly I could not sign my name on the admitting forms and I could not hold the cup of water they gave me to wash down the librium. My fingers were swollen with fluid, my face was puffy and scaly red, my liver ached, my stomach was queasy, my esophagus burned and I was 46 pounds overweight. Maybe I did have a problem. I just didn't know.*

*I agreed, at first, to stay in that hospital only four or five days. As sick as I was from alcohol, I could not, even then, allow myself to admit that alcohol itself was the primary source of all my problems. If I did that, I felt, I would be confessing that all the harm my behavior had caused was my fault. My whole life had dissolved into a process of doing things I never intended to do and not doing things I had always resolved to do, and I desperately wanted to find some other plausible explanation for failure that absolved me of the guilt. But how many excuses did I have left? I had convinced myself that I was a creative genius, misunderstood by ordinary people, but I had never created anything but common chaos. I had convinced myself that I was a great intellectual and that I drank to relieve myself of the lonely pressures caused by my gifted insights into difficulties that lesser mortals could not see. But, in fact, I had never had an original thought. I had happily agreed at one time to a psychiatrist's diagnosis that I was a manic-depressive, feeling that a certified psychosis was a more acceptable explanation of my destructiveness than was alcoholism. Almost wildly, at one time or another, I had blamed my mother, my father, the nuns, the priests, my wife, and later my girlfriend, my many jobs and bosses, my friends, my relatives, the Internal Revenue Service, the criminal justice system, and even the weather. Only alcohol had escaped my cynical judgment, for of all my desperate fears, the greatest was the idea of having to face a single day without that drug. I agreed to stay a few days only because I was so close to delirium tremens, I dared not chance another night alone. By the end of the week, when I knew I would feel better and safer, I intended to leave and start drinking all over again.*

*But during that week I was immersed in the stories of people who were recovering from the disease which they admitted had afflicted them. Very slowly, against my will in fact, I began to realize that I had not been the first traveler to that horrid hell of panic and dread from which I had spent 16 years on the run. It became clear that they had been there too, for the experiences of that God-forsaken limbo of alcoholism are so bizarre that no human imagination could counterfeit them. It became clear also that they had found a safe way out, and that they were fully confident of going back. It became clear, too, that each of them had triumphed only through total defeat and complete surrender to the truth of the disease and had risen like the Phoenix from their own ashes. Most surprising of all was the fact that they seemed content and looked happy and hopeful and confident.*

*Most of that week I had spent crying, anchored in the deep depression, and flogging myself with the whip of guilt and remorse, and truly wishing I was dead. Somehow I began to realize, at least in an embryonic and tentative way, how very sick I was. I knew I was a thoroughly beaten man and that there was no fight left in me and no place else to run. I wanted to feel like those recovering alcoholics looked.*

*Finally, with as much dignity as I could muster, trying to look like General Lee at Appomattox, I surrendered upon their terms. Still I choked on the words, my throat tightened around them, and my jaws pulsed to warn them back, but I forced them out, "Hi, my name is Mike, and...and I'm...an...alcoholic."*

*The answer was simple, "Hi, Mike! Welcome!" That's all. No thunder, no lightning, no clucking of tongues or pursed lips or hands covering the mouth, or fingers pointing shame. Just, "Hi, Mike! Welcome!"*

*By the end of the three weeks I had fully admitted to myself and to the others that I was an alcoholic, that my life had become unmanageable because of the disease, and that I was powerless to restore myself to sanity. Only by coming to the end of my rope did I come to the beginning of God. I had taken my first beer as a college freshman in a desperate attempt to overcome the grief of homesickness and I had found in that saloon the quicksand of false camaraderie and a warm sense of belonging. Among other alcoholics, I found that same lost feeling again—a sense of oneness, of rootedness, of understanding, and belongingness, this time based on genuine caring and sharing and compassionate love. I had cried when I entered the hospital, and three weeks later, I had to fight back tears at leaving.*

*In a little over two years I have attended Alcoholics Anonymous meetings in dozens of cities and several states. The fright, the remorse, and the despair are gone, as is the desire to drink. At the age of 41, I am for the first time enjoying life and rising with the sun each morning, full of hope and full of wonder, for I am among the chosen who live now on borrowed time. I don't want to waste it. Each day has all the ups and downs of any normal life, and for the first time I am learning to handle it all like a normal person.*

*My prayer was answered when I realized that I'm Mike and I'm an alcoholic, and I now feel like other people look.*

**Female, Unmarried, College Undergraduate, 22 Years Old**

*I was brought up in an upper-middle class family. Both my parents are in helping professions. My father is alcoholic but now sober. I was third born in a series of four girls.*

*During my childhood my parents had many fights and separations mostly because of my father's drinking. I was basically a happy kid but very fearful of my father when he drank. At one point his drinking drove my mother to drugs and eventually an institution. Upon her return I became very fearful of her also, but in a different way. Dad was frightening because of his power, Mom was frightening because of her fragility. They were divorced when I was about ten. I had a very low opinion of myself by this time. I became a people pleaser to my friends. My grades were not too good in school. I cried a lot in classes and found I received attention for this and began to force myself to cry in order that I could leave class and talk to the guidance counselor.*

*After grammar school I began to get very interested in pot and alcohol when in the past I had thought of it with fear and disgust. My older sister noticed my interest and she and her boyfriend got me high. I loved it. I felt free. I laughed. I spoke nonsensically. I felt I could do anything.*

*Although my mother was not alcoholic she began to go to A.A. meetings and dating men she met there. Ron and his daughters soon became part of the family. Our get-togethers consisted of drinking and smoking pot. At first they were very discrete about smoking when I was around which made me feel left out. I was too young but my sisters weren't.*

*Junior high school wasn't a happy experience. I never felt as good as the others. I wasn't popular enough and I never got the boyfriends I wanted. My grades were still mediocre and I didn't participate in school sports anymore. I knew I wasn't the best athlete and refused to be second best so I didn't try at all.*

*Not many kids smoked pot yet so I felt mature and cool. Soon though I found other kids that smoked and began to hang around them. I finally started to feel better about myself. I had more friends and was more popular.*

*Ron and my mother got married and we moved away. At first I hung around kids I didn't like much because it was better than being alone. I eventually became part of the clique I wanted to hang around with. I started to feel even better about myself. I was cool. Many of my friends were older than me so it was easy to get alcohol. I knew where to get drugs.*

*I skipped school a lot and when I was there I was high. I participated in no school activities. I began to do other drugs like acid and speed. By the time I was fifteen I had experienced blackouts, hangovers, convulsions, and was busted for possession of marijuana.*

*My family relations were almost nonexistent. My stepfather was drinking very heavily. He and my mother went on many vacations for at least a week at a time and we kids were left at home to take care of ourselves. I liked it when they were gone because I could come home at any time, have parties, and get as drunk and stoned as I wanted—not that how drunk I was mattered because I was never punished for being drunk.*

*I started to get paranoid and my thoughts of suicide had increased. Often I thought my mother was poisoning my food. I felt she and my stepfather were trying to get rid of me. I began to hate and resent my stepfather for taking my mother from me. They began to have marital problems and slept in separate bedrooms. Eventually my stepfather went into an institution. Group therapy was a joke. I wanted no part of it. I refused to say anything. I became very rebellious against my parents. I stole money from them and started to shoplift.*

*My father had quit drinking and remarried. We thought he could provide a better home for my sister and myself and so we decided to move in. I was scared to death because I knew my drinking and drug taking would have to slow down. It didn't, in fact I was high more of the time. Nothing was good. I was afraid of my father and my stepmother was boring. I had a love-hate relationship with my sister. Sometimes I would be kind to her, other times I would beat her and threaten that if she told on me I would beat her harder.*

*Eventually my father started drinking again. My stepmother's bags were packed and Kim and I decided to run away from home.*

*Kim was forced to go back with my Mom and Ron where she was terribly emotionally abused for the next five months until Ron committed suicide through an overdose of seconal. I lived with another family in a city I had previously lived in. I got into a lot of trouble with them. I was not a good influence for their daughter and I got busted again. This time for shoplifting. They forbade me to hang around with the girl I stole with after that.*

*School was a joke. I was never there completely, always stoned.*

*After Ron died I decided to go back to my mother. I didn't cry over his death. I was glad he was gone. I still am.*

*Living with my mother was crazy. I did anything I wanted. I abused her often. She bought me alcohol and pot. I was drunk all the time, stoned all the time, and didn't come home nights. I was sixteen years old. I slept with everyone and his brother as long as he was good looking. It hurt real bad.*

*My senior year of high school kind of blew by me. I wasn't there often but I seemed to attain good grades. Stoned all the time, I got into a relationship which lasted a year and a half. We were in love, I guess. My mother allowed us to sleep together in our house. My friends thought that was real cool—it was real sick. My irresponsibility where sex was concerned got me pregnant twice. After the second abortion within four months, I became very depressed and ended up quitting cosmetology school. I was drinking almost every night. No more pot or other drugs—they made me too paranoid. I had just turned eighteen.*

*I went back to live with my mother for almost a whole year except for a few months in which I lived in Florida with my boyfriend. Our relationship became more childish. The only things we really shared together were pints of rum at the movies and sex. He called me a baby for wanting to go back to my mother to save money for college. I ignored him. I became bulimic.*

*I managed to save my social security checks to pay for school. Work money went to supporting my heavy habits. I tried to stop drinking and was successful for about a week with the help of pot. I went into withdrawal. I became paranoid, I thought people were after my life, I heard voices. My mom took me to a psychologist. He referred me to the drug abuse clinic. I didn't go. I started drinking again.*

*I really wanted to do well in college. I tried my best but I didn't realize that drugs and booze engulfed my life. It was my only love, yet it didn't do for me what it used to. I still got excited about drinking but it was more a need than a want. I would battle with myself during the day to keep from drinking until the night. I was doing a lot of acid, pot, and alcohol together—a great combination. I thought I was so worldly and experienced because I tripped.*

*I had a lot of friends. It seemed the closer one was to me the more I would hurt them. I had become violent in blackouts from time to time toward close friends. I tried to hide my blackouts from my friends but wasn't too successful. I had been blacking out for years but now they had become very frequent. I'd wake up in strange places. I'd wake up with bruises all over me. I'd wake up with last night's clothing on or no clothing. Sometimes I didn't wake up. I lost my car often, my keys, my license, my head.*

*My second year of college was worse. I had suicide on the brain constantly. Paranoid all the time. I was convinced the cashiers at the small food stores knew I was bulimic, and of course, they knew I was alcoholic, but that didn't bother me. My dad had told me I was alcoholic a year earlier but I didn't care anymore. It was too much when people knew I was a pig though. That was disgusting. Paranoid—I kept the curtains closed. I didn't answer the phone. Sometimes I'd go for days without brushing my teeth or showering. I'd cross the street when someone I knew was coming my way. I'd spit at myself in the mirror, repeatedly knock my head against the wall, hit myself in the face. I was either crying or numb. I had fewer friends and no boyfriends. By the end of the year my roommate looked at me with hate and disgust. I felt awful, guilty, like a burden.*

*My Mom considered my summer a calm one. I was down on myself. I couldn't get out of bed. I was convinced it was because of the light blue curtains that gave my room a gloomy look. I spent the summer mostly by myself, lying around the pool drinking, going to bars alone, hiding in my closet.*

*My third year of school started like the others, a lot of motivation to do well, and less partying. As usual, the plan failed. Within a month I had spent an enormous amount of money on booze and drugs. I thought I had gone crazy. I had no idea my addictions had the power to drive me out of my mind. Finally, after a fairly light night of drinking and drugging, I drove home to my mother's and became hysterical. I wanted to be put away somewhere. I thought I needed a rest from reality for a while.*

*My father knew what my problem was being an alcoholic himself. I was sent into rehabilitation for four months. It was a horror show. My moods changed constantly. I was very depressed much of the time but soon I started to feel better for longer periods of time. I started to care about myself and other people. I was becoming able to listen to them. I started to accept my alcoholism.*

*I moved back in with my mother. I felt stronger but my feelings were very confused still. Somewhere in the back of my mind I knew I'd get drunk again and I still wanted to be crazy (it was the only cop-out left). I went to outpatient alcoholism counseling and as time went on I made it to fewer and fewer A.A. meetings. I started meeting my old friends in bars and soon I found myself alone with my disease. For the first time I experienced the power of my alcoholism and I got drunk again. The same old things happened, nothing had changed. I got paranoid, blackouts, violence, suicide attempt, jail.*

*I entered another alcoholism treatment program for four months. It was very painful and frightful but I experienced a lot of growth. I became much more open to try new things when in the past I thought life was in the bottle. I have fun without alcohol. I am a living miracle. I love, I respect, and I care. I have the ability to be honest with myself and others and I have real sharing friendships with others. I don't need to or have to drink or drug with the help of people I have met in A.A. After fifteen months of sobriety I actually love myself, and life gets better with every day I stay straight.*

**Female, Married, Mother, a Librarian**

*Discovering when I was an alcoholic is probably one of the most vivid moments in my life. It was Tuesday, October 11, 1978. I had slept late that morning which was my pattern then, and waited until everyone had left the house for work or school. My oldest daughter was a freshman in college in Rhode Island, and our youngest was a senior in high school. There I was 39 years old, no job, no college education, and not knowing who in the hell I was. Just like any other morning of the past three years, I proceeded downstairs to where I had hidden a bottle of sherry in the kitchen cabinet underneath the sink. Sherry was my morning drink primarily because it was cheap. I remember always pouring my drinks into a coffee mug, knowing that if anyone came home or dropped by for a visit, they would not see what I was drinking.*

*At this point in my drinking career I did not seem to worry too much if my husband came home unexpectedly for lunch, because by noon I was usually feeling no pain and things did not seem to be so bad. Occasionally he would come home but our relationship had deteriorated so badly that our conversation was very limited. Everything about him disgusted me. He was to blame for all my problems and was a major reason for my drinking, so my alcoholic thinking went. I felt smothered, gasping for freedom, but not knowing exactly what I was looking for. I thought perhaps some other person could make things right, or perhaps a good job, or perhaps new clothes. Always searching for happiness and ending up drinking to relieve the pain. Towards the end of my drinking days all kinds of physical ailments appeared and I found myself drinking more to relieve them.*

*My afternoons were spent shopping. For some reason I found comfort in being with strangers in stores. I also think that I knew if I stayed home all day that by dinnertime I would not be able to function. On these afternoons I also bought my booze. In the last two years of drinking, I spent more time thinking about alcohol and plotting where I would buy it. I always selected liquor stores that were out of town and made mental notes not to frequent them more than once a month. I would always strike up a conversation with the clerk about a special dinner party I was planning and how I knew so little about what to serve. Vodka became my drink for several reasons: (1) it was odorless—a fallacy, it smells as bad and as much as any other alcoholic drink, (2) it looked like water—true, and I put it in my coffeemug, or in juices, or in tea or in diet soda, (3) it had less calories so I thought. I gained fifteen pounds, but was never aware of the weight gain until I stopped drinking.*

*My whole life was based on lie upon lie. I remember a time when my oldest daughter was in high school and was home sick. I returned home that day and found her in her room crying. She was the first person to confront me about my drinking. The clothing bag in my closet was my ultimate hiding place for my bottles of vodka. I usually kept one at a time in there, but I was careless and had left several empty bottles as well as a full one in there. She had discovered them and asked me why they were there. I could not answer her and walked out of her room quite shaken by the idea that someone else knew my secret. Disposing of the bottles always posed a problem. We live in the country and do not have garbage pick up, so my husband made weekly trips to the local dump. What I usually did with the bottles was to wrap them in a paper bag and place them in the bottom of another brown bag and add garbage during the day on top of the bottle. I thought this was very clever, and it was until a week before I hit bottom. For some reason I had put three or four quart bottles and two half gallon bottles in the garbage in one bag. My husband had seen them, and along came the second confrontation. I had been out shopping and when I entered the kitchen there were the bottles lined up on the kitchen counter. He asked me where they came from and I remember saying I don't know. I think he thought that perhaps our oldest daughter had put them there, but I know today that he probably accepted that explanation in order to deny the fact that his wife had a problem.*

*The feelings I had when I was drinking varied greatly. In the beginning, in my early twenties, alcohol made me feel great. Most of the drinking then was strictly social and occasional. As the years progressed it increased to drinking every weekend and I was consuming more alcohol to feel that certain high. I always felt attractive, loving, and at ease with other people while I was drinking. In the last two years of my drinking, I began to hate myself and my life. I remember getting up in the morning and looking in the mirror and asking myself what is the point of getting up. I felt so useless, ugly, and very depressed. Deep down in my heart I knew I was in trouble with alcohol, but kept right on denying it with something like, only bums in the bowery are alcoholics, not me. Then I would think, what would my husband say, what would my children say, what would everyone else say? But I knew, and it even made me drink more to hide the pain of guilt and shame. I wondered often how to get off the merry-go-round my life was in but did not know how. I finally reached a point where I wanted help.*

*I recall one evening six months before the end of my drinking, my husband and I were eating dinner in a restaurant. Prior to going out to dinner, I had had several drinks and was feeling quite high. Before going out to dinner or a party I always fortified myself with plenty of alcohol. At the restaurant I had several cocktails and by the time dinner arrived I could barely see the plate in front of me much less eat the food. I remember crying and saying to my husband, I need help over and over. Perhaps something was planted that night because I remember him saying there was help and it was called A.A. I wasn't quite ready for that at the time, but later A.A. would appear more desirable to me.*

*The emotions of guilt, shame, and total isolation from everyone began to build up and I began to notice that I needed more alcohol in order to cope and to function each day. A week before I reached bottom, I remember saying, God please help me. I had not been to church in more than fifteen years, but somewhere deep inside of me I knew I needed help desperately. The help I needed had to come from a source other than myself. I knew I could not do it by myself, but who or what I was not sure.*

*On that Tuesday evening in October of 1978, I had been drinking more than usual and remember my husband calling to say he would not be home for dinner that night. I was furious with him—how dare he not come home, after all I had done in preparing a lovely meal. Feeling angry and lonely, I was so overcome with emotions, I grabbed the dinner off the stove and dumped it all over the kitchen floor. The gates of emotion opened and I got down on my knees in the middle of the kitchen floor and kept saying over and over as the tears poured, God please help me. Almost like a light being turned on, I stood up and reached for the local telephone book and looked in the classified under alcoholism information. Standing there, trembling, I reached for the telephone and dialed the number. Someone answered and all I could say was when is the next meeting. I remember the man saying tonight at 8:30 and he gave me the location. I knew where it was. I proceeded to clean the kitchen floor and pour myself another drink. I needed the drink, I told myself, in order to go to the meeting.*

*Today as I reflect on that night, it was a miracle that I arrived there safely and returned home that night safely. To me A.A. gave me back my life which I had lost through excessive drinking and nondirected living. I remember someone in the program saying we are reborn. I believe that my life began that night. A.A. taught me a whole new way of living day by day with myself and others. For me it was a very spiritual experience. I firmly believe that a person can change with help and guidance. Why the program works has been the topic of discussion and research. My own thoughts are it works for those who want it to, but even more it works for those who believe in a power or God much stronger than the individual.*

*And now, five years later, I have a full-time position of responsibility, have completed a B.A. degree, and have the love and respect of my family and friends.*

*Many rewarding moments have arisen from my being sober. I hold fast to the principles of A.A. which guide me daily in all my affairs. I like myself and have begun to formulate some new goals for myself, one of which is to go on to graduate school.*

*When I first went to that A.A. meeting five years ago, I remember saying over and over to someone there, "Why me?" I do not question anymore, I know why now. Being a recovered alcoholic is a very vital part of my being and identity as a person.*

*The desire to drink left me a long time ago and I can go to parties and other social functions where alcohol is served and enjoy myself and the company of others and be totally at ease. I could not do that before.*

# BIBLIOGRAPHY


Bailey, W., Hustmyer, F., & Kristofferson, A. (1961). Alcoholism, brain damage and perceptual dependence. *Quarterly Journal of Studies on Alcohol, 22,* 387-393.

Barnes, G. E. (1980). Characteristics of the clinical alcoholic personality. *Journal of Studies on Alcohol, 41,* 894-909.

Beckman, L. J. (1978). The self-esteem of alcoholic women. *Journal of Studies on Alcohol, 39,* 491-498.

Beckman, L. J., Day, T., Bardsley, P., & Seeman, A. Z. (1980). The personality characteristics and family backgrounds of women alcoholics. *International Journal of the Addictions, 15* (1), 47-54.

Berg, N. L. (1971). Effects of alcohol intoxication on self-concept; studies of alcoholics and controls in laboratory conditions. *Journal of Studies on Alcohol, 32,* 442-543.

Brown, R. A., & Cutter, H. S. G. (1977). Alcohol, customary drinking behavior and pain. *Journal of Abnormal Psychology, 86,* 179-188.

Buchsbaum, M. S., & Ludwig, A. M. (1981). Effects of sensory input and alcohol administration on visual evoked potentials in normal subjects and alcoholics. In H. Begletter (Ed.), *Alcohol intoxication and withdrawal.* New York: Plenum.

Button, A. D. (1956). A study of alcoholics with the Minnesota multi-phasic personality inventory. *Quarterly Journal of Studies on Alcohol, 17,* 263-281.

Cattell, R. B., Eber, H. W., & Tatsuoka, M. M. (1970). *Handbook for the sixteen personality factor questionnaire (16PF).* Champaign, IL: Institute for Personality and Ability Testing.

Chess, S. B., Neuringer, C., & Goldstein, G. (1971). Arousal and field dependency in alcoholics. *Journal of General Psychology, 85,* 93-102.

Chodorkoff, B. (1964). Alcoholism and ego function. *Quarterly Journal of Studies on Alcohol, 25,* 292-299.

Cisin, I. H., & Cahalan, D. (1968). Comparison of abstainers and heavy drinkers in a national survey. *Psychiatric Research Reports, 24,* 10-21.

Connor, R. G. (1962). The self-concepts of alcoholics. In D. J. Pittman & C. R. Snyder (Eds.), *Society, culture and drinking patterns,* New York: Wiley.

Cowan, L., Auld, F., & Begin, P. E. (1974). Evidence for distinctive personality traits in alcoholics. *British Journal of Addictions, 69,* 199-206.

Craddick, R. A., & Leipold, W. D. (1968). Note on the height of draw-a-person figures by male alcoholics. *Journal of Project Techniques, 32,* 486.

Curlee, J. (1970). A comparison of male and female patients at an alcoholic treatment center. *Journal of Psychology, 74,* 239-247.

Cutter, H. S. G., & Fisher, J. C. (1980). Family Experience and the motives for drinking. *International Journal of the Addictions, 15* (3), 339-358.

Cutter, H. S. G., Maloof, B., Kurtz, N. R., & Jones W. C. (1976). Feeling no pain, differential responses to pain by alcoholics and non-alcoholics before and after drinking. *Journal of Studies on Alcohol, 37,* 273-277.

DePalma, N., & Clayton, H. D. (1958). Scores of alcoholics on the sixteen personality factor questionnaire. *Journal of Clinical Psychology, 14,* 390-392.

Donovan, J. E., Jessor, R., & Jessor, L. (1983). Problem drinking in adolescence and young adulthood. *Journal of Studies on Alcohol, 44* (1).

Eastman, C., & Norris, H. (1982). Alcohol dependence, relapse, and self-identify. *Journal of Studies on Alcohol, 43*(11), 1214-1231.

Frey, D. & Carlock, C.J. (1984). *Enhancing self esteem.* Muncie, IN: Accelerated Development.

Fromme, K., & Samson, H. H. (1983). A survey analysis of first intoxication experiences. *Journal of Studies on Alcohol, 44* (5).

Fuller, G. B., Lunney, G. H., & Naylor, W. M. (1966). Role of perception in differentiating subtypes of alcoholism. *Perceptual and Motor Skills, 23,* 735-743.

Glatt, M. M. (1959). A chart of alcohol addiction and recovery. *British Journal of Addiction, 54* (2).

Goldstein, G., & Chotlos, J. W. (1965). Dependency and brain damage in alcoholics. *Perceptual and Motor Skills, 21,* 135-150.

Goss, A., & Morosko, T. E. (1969). Alcoholism and clinical symptoms. *Journal of Abnormal Psychology, 74,* 682-684.

Goss, A., & Morosko, T. E. (1970). Relation between a dimension of internal/external control and the MMPI with an alcoholic population. *Journal of Consulting and Clinical Psychology, 34,* 189-192.

Gross, W. F., & Alder, L. O. (1970). Aspects of alcoholics' self-concepts as measured by the Tennessee self concept scale. *Psychological Reports, 27,* 431-434.

Gynther, M. D., Presher, C. H., & McDonald, R. L. (1959). Personal and interpersonal factors associated with alcoholism. *Quarterly Journal of Studies on Alcohol, 20,* 321-333.

Hagnell, O., & Tunving, K. (1972). Mental and physical complaints among alcoholics. *Quarterly Journal of Studies on Alcohol, 33,* 77-84.

Hannon, R., Day, C. L., Butler, A. M., Larson, A. J., & Casey, M. (1983). Alcohol consumption and cognitive functioning in college students. *Journal of Studies on Alcohol, 44* (2).

Harford, T., & Spiegler, D. (1982). *Environmental influences in adolescent drinking.* National Institute on Alcohol Abuse and Alcoholism. Special Population Issues. Alcohol and Health Monograph, No. 4, D.H.H.S. Pub No. (ADM) 82-1193, Washington, D.C.: Sup. of Doc. U.S. Gov't Printing Office.

Harford, T. C., & Spiegler, D. L. (1983). Developmental trends of adolescent drinking. *Journal of Studies on Alcohol, 44* (1), 181-188.

Hawthorne, W., & Menzel, N. (1983). Youth treatment should be a programming priority. *Alcohol Health and Research World.* National Institute on Alcohol Abuse and Alcoholism, *7* (4), 46-50.

Hewitt, C. C. (1943). A personality study of alcohol addiction. *Quarterly Journal of Studies on Alcohol, 4,* 368-386.

Hoffman, H. (1970a). Depression and defensiveness in self-descriptive moods of alcoholics. *Psychological Reports, 26,* 23-26.

Hoffman, H. (1970b). Personality characteristics of alcoholics in relation of age. *Psychological Reports, 27,* 167-171.

Hubbard, R. L., Cavanaugh, E. R., Rachal, J. V., Schlenger, W. E., & Ginzburg, H. M. (1983). Alcohol use and problems among adolescent clients in drug treatment programs. *Alcohol Health and Research World.* National Institute on Alcohol Abuse and Alcoholism *7* (4), 10-18.

Imber, S. D., Miller, A. E., Faillace, L. A., & Liberman, B. (1971). Temporal processes in alcoholism. *Quarterly Journal of Studies on Alcohol, 32,* 304-309.

Jackson, D. (1957). The question of family homeostatis. *The Psychology Quarterly Supplement, 31* (1), 79-90.

Jones, M. C. (1968). Personality correlates and antecedents of drinking patterns in adult males. *Journal of Consulting and Clinical Psychology, 32,* 2-12.

Karp, S. A., Poster, D. D., & Goodman, A. (1963). Differentiation in alcoholic women. *Journal of Personality, 31,* 386-393.

Keller, M. (1980). Alcohol and youth. In J. E. & W. J. Filstead (Eds.), *Adolescence and Alcohol.* Cambridge, MA: Ballener.

Konovsky, M., & Wilsnack, S. C. (1982). Social drinking and self-esteem in married couples. *Journal of Studies on Alcohol, 43* (3) 319-333.

Kristianson, P. A. (1970). A comparison study of two alcoholic groups and control group. *British Journal of Medical Psychology, 43,* 161-175.

Laird, J. T. (1962). A comparison of male normals, psychiatric patients, and alcoholics for sex drawn first. *Journal of Clinical Psychology, 18,* 302.

Loper, R. G., Kammeier, M. L., & Hoffman, H. (1973). MMPI characteristics of college freshman males who later became alcoholics. *Journal of Abnormal Psychology, 82,* 159-162.

Machover, S., Puzzo, F. S., Machover, K., & Plumeau, F. (1959). Clinical and objective studies of personality variables in alcoholism. *Quarterly Journal of Studies on Alcohol, 20,* 528-542.

McClelland, D., & Davis, W. N. (1972). The influence of unrestrained power concerns on drinking in working class man. In D. C. McClelland, W. N. Davis, R. Kalin, & E. Wanner, *The drinking man.* New York: The Free Press.

McClelland, D. C., Wanner, E., & Vanneman, R. (1972). Drinking in the wilder context of restrained and unrestrained assertive thoughts and acts. In D. C. McClelland, W. N. Davis, R. Kalin, & E. Wanner, *The drinking man.* New York: The Free Press.

McCord, J. (1972). Etiologica factors in alcoholism; family and personal characteristics. *Quarterly Journal of Studies on Alcohol, 33,* 1020-1027

McKenna, T., & Pickens, R. (1981). Alcoholic children of alcoholics. *Journal of Studies on Alcohol, 42* (11), 1021-1029.

McKenna, T., & Pickens, R. (1983). Personality characteristics of alcoholic children of alcoholics. *Journal of Studies on Alcohol, 44* (4).

Meer, B., & Amon, A. H. (1963). Age-sex preference patterns of alcoholics and normals. *Quarterly Journal of Studies on Alcohol, 24,* 417-431.

Milman, D. H., Bennett, A. A., & Hanson, M. (1983). Psychological effects of alcohol in children and adolescents. *Alcohol Health and Research World.* World National Institute on Alcohol Abuse and Alcoholism, *7* (4).

Needle, R., McCubbin, H., Lorence, J., & Hochlauser, M. (1983). Reliability and validity of adolescent self-reported drug use in a family-based study: A methodological report. *The International Journal of Addictions, 18* (7), 901-902.

Parker, F. B. (1959). A comparison of the sex temperment of alcoholics and moderate drinkers. *American Sociological Review, 24,* 366-374.

Parker, F. B. (1969). Self-role strain and drinking disposition at a pre-alcoholic age level. *Journal of Social Psychology, 78,* 55-61.

Petrie, A. (1967). *Individuality in pain and suffering.* Chicago, IL: University of Chicago Press.

Rachal, J. V., Guess, L. L., Hubbard, R. L., Maisto, S. A., Cavanaugh, E. R., Waddell, R., & Benrud, C. H. (1983). The extent and nature of adolescent drug use. The 1974 and 1978 national sample studies. *Adolescent Drinking Behavior, 1.* Rockville, MD: National

Institute on Alcohol Abuse and Alcoholism. *Alcohol Health and Research World,* National Institute on Alcohol Abuse and Alcoholism, *7* (4), 1983.

Robins, L. N., Bates, W. M., & O'Neal, P. (1982). Adult drinking patterns of former problem children. In D. J. Pittman & C. R. Snyder (Eds.), *Society, culture and drinking patterns.* New York: Wiley.

Roos, P., & Albers, R. (1965). Performance of alcoholics and normals on a measure of temporal orientation. *Journal of Clinical Psychology, 21,* 34-36.

Sargent, M. J. (1966). Frata House, an Australian alcoholic unit. *Medical Journal of Australia, 2,* 753-757.

Sattler, J. M., & Pflugrath, J. F. (1970). Future-time perspective in alcoholics and normals. *Quarterly Journal of Studies on Alcohol, 31,* 839-850.

Segal, B., Huba, G. J., & Singer, J. L. (1980). Reasons for drug and alcohol use by college students. *International Journal of the Addictions, 15* (4), 489-498.

Shore, E. R., Rivers, P. C., & Berman, J. J. (1983). Resistance by college students to peer pressure to drink. *Journal of Studies on Alcohol, 44* (2).

Smart, R. G. (1968). Future time perspectives in alcoholics and social drinkers. *Journal of Abnormal Psychology, 73,* 81-183.

Spiegel, D., Hadley, P. A., & Hadley, R. G. (1970). Personality test patterns of rehabilitation center alcoholics, psychiatric inpatients and normals. *Journal of Clinical Psychology, 26,* 366-371.

Tahka, V. (1966). *The alcoholic personality: A clinical study, 13.* Helsinki: Finnish Foundation for Alcohol Studies.

Williams, A. F. (1965). Self-concepts of college problem drinkers. A comparison with alcoholics. *Quarterly Journal of Studies on Alcohol, 26,* 586-594.

Wisotsky, M. (1958). A note on the order of figure drawing among incarcerated alcoholics. *Journal of Clinical Psychology, 15,* 65.

Wisotsky, M., & Birner, L. (1960). Preference for human or animal drawings among normal and addicted. *Perceptual and Motor Skills, 10,* 43-45.

Witkin, H. A., Dyk, R. B., Faterson, H. F., Goodenough, D. R., & Karp, S. A. (1962). *Psychological differentiation.* New York: Wiley.

Zucker, R. A. (1968). Sex-role identity patterns and drinking behavior of adolescents. *Quarterly Journal of Studies on Alcohol, 29,* 868-884.

# Part II

# THE COUNSELOR

# PART II

# THE COUNSELOR

How effectively counseling proceeds will be determined in considerable measure by the personality which the counselor brings to the session. Quite apparently, the counselor's self-image and the image which is projected to the client will influence interaction in counseling. How secure or insecure the counselor is personally, how confident or anxious, how tolerant or judgemental will affect client reactions, responses, and outcomes.

This author's view is that the critical ingredient in counselor personality is the motivation to grow and learn. Trite but true, every client is unique. Ergo, every counseling session can and should be viewed by the counselor as a potential learning experience and as another opportunity to grow.

The person who cannot or will not take such a view ordinarily does not find reward in counseling. Such a person should give second thoughts to becoming a counselor. If such an individual is functioning in the counselor role he/she should quit. Why? Because the effective, competent counselor knows, feels that he/she does more than fill a role. *The effective counselor finds reward in serving another person.* And if the counselor does not find reward in serving, he/she will not find reward in counseling. Most assuredly, such a counselor will "burn out."

# RESEARCH FINDINGS

## Counselor Perception

How the counselor perceives the alcoholic is critical for how he/she relates to a client. The evidence is that alcoholism counselors are inclined to perceive their clients optimistically or in Hart's (1975-76) words, "in a positive and therapeutic light." There is evidence also which indicates that how the counselor perceives the client, more particularly what he/she expects of the client, will strongly influence the outcome of therapy. Leake and King (1977) found that in a study of disadvantaged alcoholics of skid-row status, those counselors were the most successful who adhered to the most optimistic expectations for their client's recovery. These findings are substantiated in a study by Talbot and Gillen (1978) who researched a comparable client population. These researchers concluded that therapeutic outcome is correlated with the perception and the values which a counselor holds.

Values according to Hertzman and Mitnick (1978-79) are a critical factor in alcoholism programs. They have recommended that ethics be included in the curricula of alcoholism training programs because value judgements are necessarily involved in every aspect of the training and evaluation of the counselor and in the treatment of the client.

## Personal and Professional Qualities

Studies in the field of counselor effectiveness indicated that the counselor's personal qualities are a more valid and fruitful area for research than are education, training, or theoretical orientation. Wrenn (1960) found that a counselor's ability to respond effectively to his/her client has little to do with the theoretical school followed. Strupp (1957) in an earlier study comparing the psychoanalytic with the client-centered approach found the same data. He felt that Wolberg, an analyst, and Rogers of the client-centered approach "were both warm, accepting, and noncritical." In short, both were comparably effective.

Carkhuff and Truax (1965) found that length of training is not necessarily an important criterion for counselor effectiveness. These researchers found that some counselors function effectively if they have undergone only one hundred hours of training.

In another earlier work Perez (1965) indicated that the effective counselor is one who meets important personal needs when he/she counsels. Prime among these needs, according to Munson (1961) is nurturance, that is to shelter emotionally and to take care of people. Mills and Abeles (1965) found that the need to like people was as important to a counselor as the need to be nurturant. In a later study with two others, Mills (1966) found that counselors also are concerned with being "warm and passionate, intuitive, and psychologically penetrating."

A study by Valle (1981) which dealt with personal qualities of the counselor found that counselors who relate easily and well, who find it easy to be empathic, who are basically genuine and straightforward, have a lower rate of recidivism among their alcoholic patients than do those counselors who are not as interpersonally competent.

One of the more comprehensive studies in the area of counselor characteristics was done by Menne (1975). With the help of seventy-five experienced therapists, he drew up a questionnaire which listed one hundred and thirty-two counselor qualities. Over three hundred and fifty counselors responded to his research instrument. The four highest ranked qualities concerned:

1. **Professional ethics.** The counselor's personal conduct in the therapeutic relationship was given number one priority.

2. **Self-awareness.** This quality particularly as relates to competency, attitudes, prejudices, and limitations ranked second.

3. **Personal characteristics.** These were ranked third. These qualities focused upon maturity, flexibility, respect for clients, and intuitiveness.

4. **The ability to listen and communicate.** That this quality should rank so high reflects this counselor's conviction about its importance.

These findings may be interpreted to mean that the effective, professional counselor is a person of conscience. Now that ethics are an integral part of conscience is obvious. But if one reflects upon the other three findings by Menne (1975), they too, are aspects of conscience. Why? Because they all reflect the extent to which one is emotionally identified and concerned with others. Self-awareness, as defined in this book, is premised upon interpersonal relationships as is respect, maturity, and even, perhaps especially, the ability to listen and communicate.

Another way to interpret these findings is that the counselor is one who finds reward in giving, in helping others. Apparently by helping others, the counselor helps him/herself. Riessman (1965) found this to be true and in a study more than a decade later Rakos and Schroeder (1976) came to the same conclusion.

## SELECTED COUNSELOR RESPONSES

Studies are critical because they provide data which is detached and authoritative. At the same time the counseling process itself is quite the opposite. It is warm, dynamic, and more often than not, emotional. This is especially true when one counsels the alcoholic.

In order to inject some warmth, even human interest into the discussion, the author asked five experienced, practicing counselors of alcoholics to respond to the following questions.

1. What are the most important qualities which make for an effective counselor of alcoholics?

2. How do you perceive the alcoholic?

3. What personal qualities do you seek to exhibit when you counsel the alcoholic?

4. What professional qualities do you deem to be most important when you counsel the alcoholic?

Counselor responses follow:

**Response from a Female, Forty-two Years Old, Five Years Experience, M.A.**

*I see the alcoholic as a person suffering from an incurable illness which can be arrested if the use of alcohol is discontinued.*

*This can be done. I know it because I've seen alcoholics recovered. I also bear in mind that he/she is a very sensitive and fragile person who needs to develop a balance in his/her life to cope with feelings.*

*I try to show care and love. I try to be warm yet direct too. I share. I share my thoughts and experiences.*

*I try to show my clients that I know about the deviance of alcoholism. I try to show them that I accept them but not their drunkeness. I stay in touch with their feelings. Mostly I show them that I am nonjudgemental. Alcoholic clients have been judged enough, especially by themselves.*

*I've always believed that to have communication with an alcoholic client you must show your wholeness as a person and you must share in appropriate terms your own self.*

**Male, Fifty Years Old, Ten Years Experience, Recovering Alcoholic**

(This counselor preferred to be interviewed rather than to write his responses. The material is derived from an edited tape.)

*I deal with drinkers, not alcoholics. A person comes in because he has a drinking problem not because he is an alcoholic. I hate labels. But that's not the only reason I differentiate between a person who's uncomfortable with his drinking and an alcoholic. The word alcoholic terrifies people, especially one who got the courage to walk in here. Why scare him away, and I would if I saw and referred to him as an alcoholic. So I see each person who comes in as a* **person** *who's got a drinking problem, and how bad the drinking problem is got nothing to do with how often I see him or he wants to see me. All that doesn't mean much, in fact I think it's irrelevant. When I counsel I'm totally honest (I like to think I'm like that all the time). There's no bluff in my counseling. The counselor who bluffs will get nowhere. He might just as well close shop. See, a bluffer is the easiest guy to con. And drinkers, my friend, are masters of the con.*

*I learned a long time ago that I do my best counseling when I share my own story. I'm very direct and I don't soften my words, but what I never do is put the person on the defensive. I never attack him, I never judge him. What I try to communicate is two things: (1) like him, I'm trying to beat the booze, I'm in the same boat he is; and (2) it's a life-time battle.*

*Professional qualities—the two most important ones are empathy—let him know that you share his world, yeah, you've walked in his moccasins; and also listening. I mean* **listening**—*you know God made two ears but only one mouth. The counselor should listen twice as much as he talks. He should always let the client identify his own problem. To try to do that for him is the surest way I know to drive him away.*

**Male, Twenty-Four Years Old, Two Years Experience, M.A., C.A.G.S.**

*I perceive alcoholics as individuals who are in much pain. A person who feels completely hopeless and who has lost touch with his values, who's thinking is distorted and does not know why.*

*The behavior that an active alcoholic displays is behavior that often times is in direct conflict with his values. This, I believe causes an astronomical amount of guilt and remorse.*

*Because I believe the previous statement, I feel the most precious, most fundamental quality that is needed by an alcoholism counselor, would be that of complete acceptance. An active alcoholic, a person who is "new" to treatment (booze free) feels "bad," guilty, and involved in behaviors that seem to have no rational explanation. They need to be accepted, not judged (They are their harshest judges anyway). Compassion is vital. Then after these traits have been established guilt reduction ensues and value clarification can follow. In time, the recovering alcoholic can then learn to accept his illness, thus begin to see the rewards that come from values that are clarified. This hopefully keeps alcoholics sober.*

*I feel I most need to remain compassionate yet detached, congruent—consistent, yet empathic. These qualities I try very hard to display to the alcoholic. I must constantly be aware/be cautious of over-identification with the alcoholic. This is difficult because it is much easier to be human and to display human qualities than be a professional trying to reduce pain via the professional guidelines. The two—human compassion and professional sensitivity—have a fine line separating them. Nonetheless, it is a boundary which must be adhered to for maximum effect.*

**Female, Thirty-Nine Years Old, Five Years Experience, M.A. in Psychology, L.C.S.W.**

*The most important qualities which makes for an effective counselor are empathy and acceptance of the client where he/she is. The ability to give guidance through options open to the client and in an in-patient setting to provide a positive role is critical as a counselor is more visible in his/her humaneness.*

*While a college degree with a major in psychology is useful, I feel that empathy and a counselor's own personal growth is essential in counseling the alcoholic as in other counseling. While the need is to be objective, also a need is for genuine compassion. It is important that the counselor not be controlling but accepting.*

*These clients need as do other clients to be viewed in a holistic manner—spiritually, physically, and psychologically. Value clarifications are important for some clients and others issue around sexuality, some ask for spiritual guidance. It is a "no no" generally in the field of psychology to deal with the spiritual realm, but A.A. talks of "Our Higher Power" and feels that sobriety is based on giving over their disease to God. Some are not ready to deal with this, others want to understand.*

*As counselors, I feel we must help these individuals find their own answers as to how they can relate to their God. There is no need to go into depth, there are others in the religious life who can be of assistance in that area. It has to be understood that alcoholism leaves clients with a loss of values and habits which they would never have chosen sober because of the nature of the disease. This leaves them with a tremendous amount of guilt and self-anger. It cannot be ignored. Along with this, a client needs to be treated with respect and supported in building a more positive self-image.*

*They need to be provided with as much information on the disease as possible along with available resources for support in the community. A counselor should look at the clients positive points and build on these. You may find a great deal of artistic talents. Many are highly intelligent and creative people. Looking at their recreation and past hobbies is also important. Many have lost sight of a healthy balance in their work and play life. lost their job skills or are in need of guidance for the future.*

*Vocational counseling is essential for those who have lost their job skills or are in need of guidance for the future.*

*Socially, they either have lost the knack or never had it in the first place, they need to see that it is a basic need for all of us and they need to begin work on interpersonal relationships. Those are essential for survival in the real world without alcohol.*

*For some the sexual drive has been affected and they may need reassurance and understanding in this area. Others may need further professional help.*

*Again the whole person must be treated but as an "individual" with individual needs. The family also has needs and Al Anon is most effective. There are times when out-patient care should be considered for the alcoholic.*

*The twelve steps of A.A. are a beautiful way of life not only for alcoholics but also for all of us as human beings. I feel alcoholics who seek treatment for their disease are the most courageous human beings. They find the need and face the dark side which we all possess in order to begin the process of completely changing their lives. They painfully have to accept their disease, possibly change their environment, friendships, lifestyles, and behaviors almost immediately and simultaneously. They live with the fear of death should they again pick up that one drink. They see the poor recovery rate and wonder if they are going to make it. They are told they have to attend A.A. weekly, that there are no simple answers to maintain sobriety. There are other options but the success rate is much poorer. They find their families are possible enablers, that they too have become sick in living with the alcoholic. They need to know that their attitude can change the relations and attitudes around, that the "glass is half full."*

*Each patient I work with, as Sheldon Kopp says, is a journey for me into another world. It is a privilege and obligation for me to do the best I can. Therefore, I as the counselor have an obligation to stay healthy and to grow emotionally, as well as intellectually. I believe too that you must, as the Indian Prayer says, be aware that you do not know someone unless you have walked in their mocassins. It is important for me to see the patient through his/her eyes and assist him/her in building up his/her fragile ego. That's primary to treatment. The program in which I counsel is thirty days in length and is scheduled in eight sessions. It is difficult to go beyond secondary withdrawal and confusion. Some patients can get into insight work, others not. I look for most clients to seek further treatment through outpatient work and/or halfway house and A.A. support. Their strength is obvious in their incredible ability to have survived thus far and their courage to try ONE MORE TIME, A DAY or A MOMENT AT A TIME. When I think of the tremendous energy needed for me to change one negative behavior in my life and then see the alcoholic attempt so many more, I cannot help be in awe of the "Spirit of the Individual."*

**Male, Fifty-Nine Years Old, Thirty-Four Years Experience. M.Ed.**

*There are many teachers, few Socrates. There are many physicians, few Schweitzers. There are many religious, few Luthers or Sisters Theresa.*

*I guess what I'm trying to say is that in alcoholism counseling, the most effective therapy begins in the nail-beds of the counselor's and client's toes and spreads thence to every cell of the body physical, mental, and spiritual. It is true holism, wherein something greater than the sum of the parts is hoped for.*

*Quite obviously, love, genuineness, and empathy must be internalized realities of the therapist's substance. Unfortunately, empathy is best learned in the street, feeling the pain of an empty belly, and the slow dying of hope. Yet it is from this human condition that the indigent drug abuser frequently comes.*

*Lofty intellectualism has little or no place in working with the disenfranchized and disenchanted alcoholic. It is an added slur to his/her desperate deprivation, alienation, and isolation. Squalor neither sees an exquisite sunset nor experiences the joy of a Goya hung in the local museum. This sort of thing is better left in the hallowed halls of learning.*

*I don't mean to imply that a solid working knowledge of psychological theorists is not desirable; it is indispensable. Also of indispensability is a solid working knowledge of the Fellowship of Alcoholics Anonymous, historically perhaps the most available, inexpensive, and effective therapy since alcoholism began to emerge from the dark-ages of ignorance and bias a mere 50 years ago.*

*It has been this writer's experience that needs of the patient are best served if both ongoing counseling and A.A. participation are utilized concurrently rather than sequentially. Assisting the patient to identify, assess, better understand, and then modify unhealthy emotions which frequently contribute to the development and/or perpetuation of addiction is essential and traditionally the role of the counselor, psychologist, or psychiatrist. The philosophy, teachings, and activity of Alcoholics Anonymous provide daily availability and continuity of community, socialization, nonjudgemental support, compassion, and role modeling. The process of recovery should be hastened by making available to the patient the "best of both worlds" (hopefully), professional as well as para-professional.*

*P.S. I always counsel with this thought feeling:*

***Humble love, and not proud science keeps the door of heaven.***

Young

The previous five responses reflect a number of common denominators in perception and in personal and professional qualities.

**An Analysis—Counselor Perception**

Counselors, like subjects in research findings, tend to perceive optimistically. They believe alcoholics can recover. They focus on positive qualities and "build on these." The first counselor noted that the illness "can be arrested if he discontinues the use of alcohol" and went on to say, "This can be done. I know it . . . ."

Counselors perceive realistically too. Thus counselors one and three observed that the alcoholic is a fragile person "who is in a great deal of pain. A person who feels completely hopeless and who has lost touch with his own values, whose thinking is distorted . . . ." What this all means is that both an optimistic and realistic perception are needed if a counselor is going to be effective.

The counselor's perception is characterized also by a need to share the client's perception. These counselors know that they can't themselves change the alcoholic. *He/she* must want to change. The starting point for this change they feel is in communicating to the client that they want to share his view of the world.

**Counselor Personal Qualities**

Counselors recognize that they can accomplish change if they *share* themselves. The first counselor put it very succinctly "I share. I share my thoughts and my experiences." The second counselor put it just as aptly another way, "what I try to do is to communicate that "I'm in the same boat he is. I'm trying to beat the booze." Emotional sharing to this author means emotional investment. It is when he/she is able to communicate these feelings that the effective counselor feels that dividends are received from their emotional investment. And what are the dividends? They are rich and precisely, the counselor's knowledge that the client no longer feels alone in despair and threat which he/she perceives.

What other qualities do these counselors deem important? *Authenticity* seems to be among the top ones, "When I counsel I'm totally honest . . . There's no bluff in my counseling." Complete *acceptance* of the alcoholic person is another. This acceptance seems to stem from another quality, namely: *compassion.* These counselors seem able to incorporate both qualities because they've learned to distinguish between the person of the alcoholic and the behavior. They accept him/her, not the drinking. Inextricably interwoven with these qualities is a strong penchant for *nurturance.* Nurturant counselors are those who are interested, who care, and who are motivated to help.

**Professional Qualities**

Despite these personal qualities of nurturance, compassion, acceptance, and sharing, counselors believe that the effective counselor is one who must remain cognitively detached from the counseling. When one remains so, the counselor is able to listen and to respond better. Equally important, only by maintaining this detachment, will the counselor be able to maintain an appropriate perspective of the counseling relationship. This quality is what one counselor was referring to when he wrote, "I constantly must be aware/be cautious of overidentification with the alcoholic." What this counselor recognizes is that when he/she overidentifies with the client, he/she is responding to his/her own needs and not those of the client. When the counselor becomes overidentified with the client *he/she is in danger of destroying the therapeutic relationship.* When overidentification occurs, counselors invariably fall prey to their own feelings. They become overwhelmed by the client's emotions and demands. They lose the ability to listen and interpret the true meaning of the client's feelings. Their perception becomes so clouded that the person of the client becomes major for them, the behavior (alcoholism) minor, or they become unable to distinguish between the two at all. In order to meet counselor needs (perhaps justify the feelings of supposed love for the client) the counselor often lets him/herself be sucked into the client's psychological defenses, denying or rationalizing the client's alcoholism. Under circumstances such as these the counselor's perception becomes so distorted that he/she loses sight of the basic purpose of the counseling—to meet the needs of the client. In sum, if counselors are not careful about maintaining their cognitive detachment they risk losing their integrity both as counselors and as persons.

Finally, the quality, personal-professional, which seemed to transcend the personalities of these counselors, was their pensiveness. These are thinking people, who unquestionably have a bent for introspection. Consider some of their lines, ". . . you must show your wholeness as a person." "It is much easier to be human and to display human qualities than to be a professional trying to reduce pain via professional guidelines." "When I think of the tremendous energy needed for me to change one negative behavior in my life and then see alcoholics attempt so many more, I cannot help be in awe." "Squalor neither sees an exquisite sunset nor experiences the joy of a Goya hung in the local museum." Thoughts like these are an important ingredient in functioning as an effective counselor.

## TRAINING OF THE COUNSELOR

### Some Prefatory Comments

Counselor training is as important as his/her personal and professional qualities. But while the literature abounds with statistical research about these latter and about the nature and treatment of alcoholism, there are few studies, statistical or even descriptive which concern the training of the counselor of alcoholics. What this author has learned, however, is that the paucity of reporting does not reflect what's happening. Indeed, what he discovered via telephone and mail is that training programs are conducted in virtually every institutional setting where alcoholism is treated. Most institutions in which alcoholism is treated view counselor training as an integral part of their total activity. These training programs vary in scope and depth and at all treatment levels. Many institutions offer intense orientations for volunteer counselors. Even more offer regularly scheduled classroom didactic work for paraprofessionals during their working shift. These didactics frequently are offered in conjunction with or to supplement courses offered by private colleges, state colleges, or university extension services. Many institutions have visiting lecturers come several times each month for the professional staff.

The variance of offerings reflects the prevailing view about alcoholism counseling, namely, that it is an ongoing process where fresh useful research about its nature and treatment constantly is being uncovered for all types and levels of counselors. And in alcoholism counseling there does seem to be a veritable myriad of types and levels of counselors.

They come from all the helping professions. Thus, in most institutional settings for alcoholics, one will find nurses, psychologists, physicians, social workers, school guidance counselors, and teachers. Some of these professionals have impeccable credentials in counseling, some have few, if any. Then too, many who work with alcoholics have relatively little formal education or formal backgrounds in counseling. In no area of mental health is there more disparity in education and training than in alcoholism counseling.

This author does not view this situation with alarm, or even with concern. Rather he views the issue of the professional counseling background of counselor of alcoholics in the same way Haley (1971) views the family therapist's background. On this topic Haley (1971) once wrote, "A therapist is now often judged on his merit—the success of his therapy—not upon his professional background." This view seems especially appropriate for the counselor of alcoholics. For generations alcoholics were treated most successfully not by professionals from medicine, psychology, social work, or education, but by counselors from Alcoholics Anonymous. In Figure 2.1 are provided some interesting data about the make-up of Alcoholics Anonymous and reflects the very considerable impact which A.A. has made upon alcoholism counseling.

Alcoholism counselors have come from a kaleidoscope of vocations and in many instances vocations which had little to do with mental health. Many of these nonprofessionals knew what the professionals refused to accept or even to see, that alcoholism is uniquely different from any other form of mental health illness. The recovering alcoholic who served as counselors knew that generations ago, and even though they might have been lacking in formal education or training in counseling, their perception of the illness and of the client, served to mitigate any professional deficiencies. Why? Because they knew possibly they could establish rapport more quickly and empathize far more effectively with the alcoholic than any professional nonalcoholic because they had themselves *experienced* the client's illness. What is most surprising to this author is that the research supporting the recovering alcoholic counselor's view is startlingly recent. Argeriou and Manohar in a 1978 study found that recovering alcoholics were far more effective with

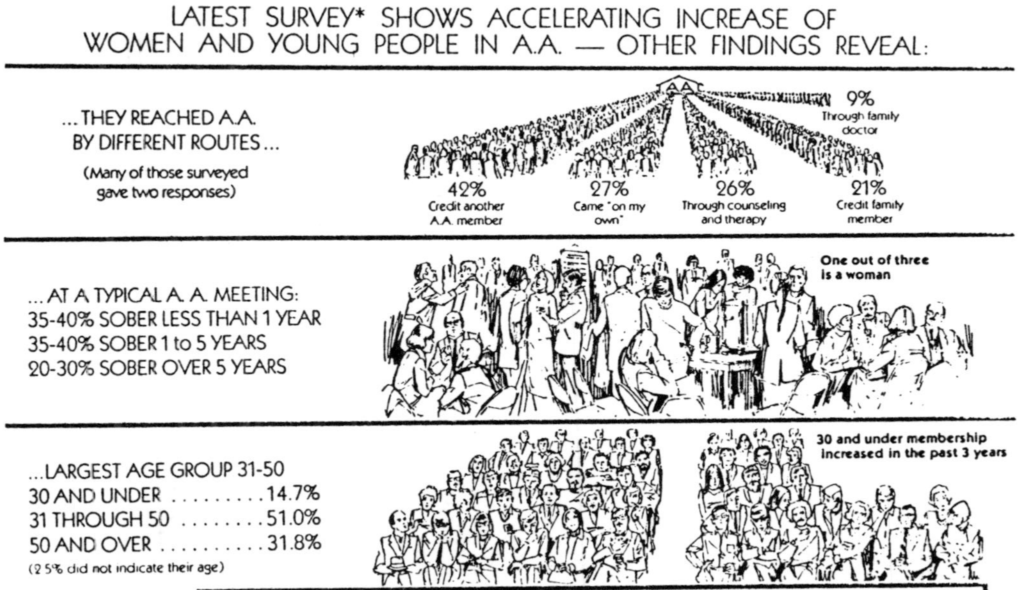


| RESPONDENTS FELL INTO THE FOLLOWING GENERAL CATEGORIES: | | Sales & Business | Homemaker | Professional | Labor | Office & Clerical | Unemployed | Retired | Other |
|---|---|---|---|---|---|---|---|---|---|
| | MEN | 19% | 0.1% | 17% | 30% | 3% | 7% | 12% | 12% |
| | WOMEN | 11% | 25% | 18% | 7% | 15% | 9% | 5% | 10% |

*Almost 25,000 A.A. members participated in the largest and most comprehensive study of its kind

Figure 2.1 Data related to Alcoholics Anonymous members. **Note.** Reprinted by permission, **The A.A. Member** (1981), Alcoholics Anonymous World Services, Inc., New York.

young drinkers than were nonalcoholic counselors. Lawson (1982) substantiated these findings with a study published four years later. He found that a history of alcoholism in the counselor promoted the therapeutic relationship. Invariably the alcoholics rated this counselor higher than the nonalcoholic counselor.

It is important to note here that these studies do not mean that a nonalcoholic cannot be an effective counselor of alcoholics. Perhaps the most important meaning to be derived from these studies is that a recovering alcoholic has an advantage over a nonalcoholic counselor precisely because of what has always been known about counseling in general. *The more positively the client perceives the counselor, the more productive the therapeutic relationship will be.*

**Research Findings**

Whatever one's position might be regarding the counselor's professional counseling background there is a uniform view by institutional staffs and administrators that ongoing inservice training is beneficial. The research supports the validity of this view. Skuja and Schneidmuhl (1975) studied the effects of an intense training program upon forty-one alcoholism trainees after seven weeks and again after fourteen weeks. At the seventh week juncture and again after fourteen weeks these researchers found a significant increase in trainee competence, in utilization in alcoholism work, personal involvement, responsibility, and overall job performance. Hoffmann and Bonyge (1977) did a study with sixteen female alcoholics who entered a nine month training program to assess the effects of the program upon their personalities. They found that the nine months of training (the emphasis was upon personal confrontation and self-awareness) helped these female counselors to become more task oriented and accepting of sympathy from others. Wehler and Hoffman (1978) compared the scores of fourteen female alcoholism counselors on the Personal Orientation Inventory before and after a nine month training program. These women scored significantly higher after the program in such areas as spontaneity, capacity for intimate contact, self-regard, and feeling reactivity. There was also a stronger bent for personal self-actualization among the subjects after the training program.

**Functional Programs**

Manohar (1973) has described a program for training volunteers. It involves ten weeks of classroom work and fifty weeks at forty hours a week of work in an alcoholism clinic under professional supervision. During the forty hour week the trainees also attended seminars and staff meetings. In a previous journal report Wilson (1968) felt that alcoholism training programs need to employ not only the traditional counseling one-on-one approach but should also train counselors in psychodrama, group therapy, and videotaping.

These two reports reflect the trend toward competency oriented programs because of the acute need for counselors. Brammer and Springer (1971) have described just such a program, designed and implemented in Washington state. In this program, performance objectives are developed and spelled out. The counselor applies and is assessed. The decision is then made whether to recommend him/her for certification or a skill training program. If he/she is certified, the counselor continues into "Lifelong professional development." If the counselor chooses to enter the skill training program, he/she does so and is subject to reassessment at the end of it and presumably state certification.

## A Recommended Program

The previous two programs and the several dozen unpublished ones which the author has studied have commonalities. They include both theory and practice. Not all, however, assess their applicants as to current level of functioning in either theory or practice. It is the author's conviction that an assessment period would be ultimately beneficial to both the trainee and the institution. Criteria and length would be determined by needs of the setting. Ideally the program should be counselor centered and its curriculum and length determined by the counselor's performance.

**Stage One—Theory.** Readings, discussion, and assessment in the following areas:

- Personality Theories—Freud, Jung, Adler, Rogers
- Abnormal Psychology
- The Alcoholic Personality
- Selected Theories and Techniques of Counseling
- Group Dynamics

**Stage Two—Practice.** This period could begin concurrently with stage one or many weeks after the onset of stage one. The variable would be the entering level of trainee sophistication in stage one.

Purposes of Stage Two are two-fold:

—To increase the trainee's own sense of awareness.

—To teach him/her counseling skills.

Accordingly, at Stage Two experiences would include:

- Doing individual counseling under videotaping. If this is not possible, then by tape recorder. Recordings would be discussed with a mentor supervisor.
- Role playing with the mentor supervisor. The trainee could alternate roles between the alcoholic client and the counselor.
- Working as a co-facilitator with a staff member experienced in group dynamics.

## THE NEW COUNSELOR

Counseling is a very personal and private enterprise. To a very great extent it is a function of personality. How it is done finally is up to you, the particular counselor.

All the foregoing research findings, explanations, and counselor views are presented for your critical examination. What implications they have for you and your counseling is dependent upon you. Quite apparently, they can be accepted and injected into your developing, counseling system or they can be rejected out of hand—your choice. The ultimate criterion for what you accept or reject has to be what fits and works for you. For in your counseling, *you are the ultimate technique.* This is a heavy responsibility because for your client, at least, you are the personification of the counseling process.

To live up to your client's expectations and more importantly, to your own, you will need to strive for excellence. Striving for excellence in counseling is a life-long process and it involves constant self-examination. If you are going to strive for excellence in your work, you will need to operate from a solid frame of reference so that you will be able to articulate, to yourself and if need be to others, your philosophy of counseling.

The following list of questions are intended as guidelines to help you develop your own philosophy.

**Guidelines for Developing a Personal Philosophy of Counseling**

1. What is your definition of counseling?

2. What are the appropriate goals of counseling?

3. How would you define your own role as a helper?

4. What are the most important functions of a counselor?

5. What are the personal qualities which make for a competent therapist?

6. What makes for a therapist's excellence? What distinguishes a mediocre from an outstanding therapist?

7. What are the main values you live by? How did those values become yours? How might those central values influence you as a helping person?

8. About what are some of your beliefs and attitudes:

    a. religion, politics, women's liberation

    b. sex outside of marriage, abortion, marriage, alternative lifestyles

    c. neglect of the aged, welfare, using drugs

    d. How can any or all the previous help or hinder your work?

9. How would you define or describe "the good life?"

10. Why are you selecting work in one of the helping professions? What is in it for you personally? What needs of yours are being met by being a "helping person?"

11. How do you view your own level of functioning? What makes you think you can be of value in assisting others in resolving their struggles?

## SUMMARY AND CONCLUSIONS

Counseling will proceed productively when the counselor is able to view each session as an opportunity to grow and to learn. The effective counselor is one who finds reward in serving another person.

Research indicates that counselors perceive their clients optimistically. Counselor expectations and values influence the outcomes of therapy.

Education, training, and theoretical orientation of a counselor seem to have little impact on counselor effectiveness. Personal and professional qualities, however, seem to be of critical importance. Chief among these are conscience from which are derived a sense of ethics, self-awareness, respect, maturity, and the ability to listen and communicate. Counselors find reward in giving probably because by giving to others they also help themselves.

The perception, personal, and professional qualities of the five practicing counselors seemed to gibe with the research findings. Thus, these counselors perceived optimistically but realistically too. They seek to share the client's perception of the world so that he/she won't feel alone in the despair and threat which he/she perceives. Authenticity, acceptance, compassion, and nurturance are also the important qualities which these counselors incorporate into their personalities.

The most salient professional quality of the counselor is cognitive detachment. Only by remaining so will the counselor be able to maintain a healthy perspective of the counseling relationship. Should he/she lose this detachment and become overidentified with the client, the counselor will jeopardize his/her professional and personal integrity. The counselors also reflected a healthy penchant for introspection.

The paucity of research on the training of alcoholism counselors does not reflect what is really going on. Most institutions treat training as an integral part of the total activity. Quite rightly, training is provided at all counselor levels and training seems to have a more positive effect on the treatment of the alcoholic than do the credentials of the counselor.

An effective training program is one which includes both theory and practice. The theory should include traditional clinical didactics and the practice should focus on developing the trainee's sense of awareness and provide him/her with the opportunity to develop basic counseling skills.

Counseling is a very personal and private enterprise. What new counselors finally accept for theory and technique will be determined by what fits and works for them. All developing counselors should operate from a frame of reference so that they can articulate especially to themselves their personal philosophy of counseling.

## TOPICS FOR DISCUSSION AND REFLECTION

1. How do you perceive the alcoholic?

2. What are your most salient, personal strengths, and how will they benefit your client?

3. In which areas do you feel professionally strong? In which deficient?

4. Which aspect of training do you enjoy the most? The least? Why?

# BIBLIOGRAPHY

Argeriou, M., & Manohar, V. (1978). Relative effectiveness of nonalcoholics and recovered alcoholics as counselors. *Journal of Studies on Alcohol, 39* (5), 793-799.

Brammer, L. M., & Springer, H. C. (1971). A radical change in counselor education and certification. *Personnel and Guidance Journal, 49* (6), 806.

Carkhuff, R. R., & Truax, C. B. (1965). Training in counseling and psychotherapy: An evaluation of an integrated didactic and experiential approach. *Journal of Consulting Psychology, 29,* 333-336.

Haley, J. (1971). Family therapy: A radical change. In *Changing families: A family therapy reader.* New York: Greene and Stratton.

Hart, L. (1975-76). Attitudes toward alcoholism among a group of rehabilitation counselors: An exploratory study. *Drug Forum, 5* (2), 139-142.

Hertzman, M., & Mitnick, L. (1978-79). Ethics, evaluation and training in alcoholism. *Drug Forum, 7* (2), 145-154.

Hoffman, H., & Bonyge, E. R. (1977). Personalities of female alcoholics who became counselors. *Psychological Reports, 41* (1), 37-38.

Lawson, G. (1982). Relation of counselor traits to evaluation of the counseling relationship by alcoholics. *Journal of Studies on Alcohol, 43* (7), 834-839.

Leake, G., & King, A. (1977). Effect of counselor expectations on alcoholic recovery. *Alcohol, Health and Research World, 1* (3), 16-22.

Manohar, V. (1973). Training volunteers as alcoholism treatment counselors. *Quarterly Journal of Studies on Alcohol, 34* (3), 869-877.

Menne, J. M. (1975). A comprehensive set of counselor competencies. *Journal of Counseling Psychology, 22* (6), 547-553.

Mills, D. J., & Abeles, N. (1965). Counselor needs for affiliation and nurturance as related to liking for clients and counseling process. *Journal of Counseling Psychology, 12,* 353-358.

Mills, D. H., Chestnut, W. H., & Hartzell, J. P. (1966). The needs of counselors: A component analysis. *Journal of Counseling Psychology, 1341,* 82-84.

Munson, J. (1961). *Patterns of Client Resistiveness and Counselor Response Dissertation Abstracts, 21,* 2368-2369.

Perez, J. F. (1965). *Counseling: Theory and practice.* Reading, MA: Addison-Wesley.

Rakos, R. F., & Schroeder, H. E. (1976). Fear reduction in help-givers as a function of helping. *Journal of Counseling Psychology, 23* (5), 428-435.

Riessman, F. (1965). The "helper therapy" principle. *Social Work, 10,* 27-32.

Skuja, A. T., Schneidmuhl, A. M., & Mandell, W. (1975). Alcoholism counselor trainees: Some changes in job related functioning following training. *Journal of Drug Education, 5* (2), 151-157.

Strupp, H. H. (1957). A multi-dimensional comparison of therapist activity in analytical and client centered therapy. *Journal of Counseling Psychology, 21,* 293-312.

Talbot, J., & Gillen, C. (1978). Differences between nonprofessional recovering alcoholic counselors treating bowery alcoholics: A study of therapist variables. *Psychiatric Quarterly, 50* (4), 333-342.

Valle, S. K. (1981). Interpersonal functioning of alcoholism counselors and treatment outcome. *Journal of Studies on Alcohol, 42* (9), 783-790.

Wehler, R., & Hoffmann, H. (1978). Personal orientation inventory scores on female alcoholism counselors before and after training. *Psychological Reports, 43* (2), 500-502.

Wilson, W. M. (1968). Hospitalized alcoholic patients: Training personnel to work with alcoholic patients. *Hospital and Community Psychiatry, 19* (7), 211-215.

Wrenn, R. L. (1960). Counselor orientation: Theoretical or situational. *Journal of Counseling Psychology, 7,* 40-45.

# Part III

# SOME THEORETICAL CONCERNS

PART **III**

# SOME THEORETICAL CONCERNS

As noted in Part II, the effective counselor is the one who finds reward in serving another person. Unfortunately, this valuable quality is sometimes mitigated in the new counselor by a Florence Nightingale—like zeal and expectation that he/she will cure all clients.

The beginning counselor should know what the experienced one learned very early, there are no cures in alcoholism counseling. There *is,* however, a recovery process. And this process can be both effective and productive if the client stops drinking. *The stopping is done by the client,* not the counselor. The counselor must bear in mind and constantly, that finally it is the client's choice to stop drinking. No amount of badgering, no amount of condescension, haranguing, or pep talks by the counselor will accomplish that, only the client can do that.

# TREATABLE AND UNTREATABLE

As many reasons exist as to why alcoholics stop drinking as there are alcoholics. All these reasons have this common denominator, namely they are born out of a sense of desperation.

**Bottom**

Among alcoholics exists phenomena termed *"high bottom," "low bottom,"* even, *"middle bottom."* Alcoholics "bottom out" when they find drink no longer provides any solutions for their desperation. At this juncture most alcoholics perceive only two alternatives—death or treatment.

Each alcoholic arrives at his/her "bottom" differently and for different reasons. For example, the middle class housewife who is still very much intact materially feels she has lost love and respect of her children. She seeks help—a high "bottom."

Another example is a male executive who loses not only his children, but his spouse, his friends, and all his material possessions. One day he finds himself on skid-row or awakens in a state hospital "loaded-up" on thorazine. He seeks help—a "low bottom."

While the level and nature of the "bottom" varies with the person, it always embraces the alcoholic's entire dynamic system. Perception, defenses, and values are always affected. Despite these variances from person to person however, there is a common denominator for all alcoholics in "the bottom"—it is the beginning of treatment.

Only when alcoholics experience their private "bottom" (and of course not all do) can they themselves appreciate their own cry *"Help me!"* And it is only when an alcoholic says to the counselor "help me" and the counselor *believes him/her,* only then is the client ready to start the psychotherapeutic journey to sustained recovery.

It should be noted that there are alcoholics who are not good candidates for psychotherapy. These include the hard core sociopath who is incapable of trust, the person afflicted with Korsakoff's syndrome, the individual who is so deficient intellectually that he/she cannot retain cognitive or affective meaning from session to session, the psychotic who suffers from flattened affect, and so forth; such alcoholics are the exception. The author's conviction is that "bottomed out" alcoholics can profit and mightily, from emotional self-examination via psychotherapy. How effective this self-examination will be is a function of the counselor's technique and skill. It is to these concerns that Part III and Part IV of this book are addressed.

# GOALS

Goals are a basic issue in counseling. Wolberg (1954) believed that they are critically important because the success or failure of the counseling can be assessed only in terms of the understood objectives. Patterson (1963) believed that the general goal of counseling is for the client to become "responsible, independent, and self-actualizing." Rogers (1961) believed that a prime purpose of counseling is to help clients become "more similar to the idea which he/she has chosen." Goals which Kanner (1963) deems appropriate for children apply to adults too. The goal of counseling he believed is to "relieve, relate, release, relearn, and relax." On reflection they seem especially apt for the alcoholic.

## Primary Goal

**The primary goal in counseling alcoholics is achievement of a *continuing sobriety.*** There are other goals too, however. These are secondary goals which are important because they facilitate the process toward the primary one and equally important, help them to adhere to it.

## Secondary Goals

1. **To help clients learn all there is to know about their alcoholism.** For motivated clients this is achieved fairly easily because the objective is primarily cognitive in nature. Regular attendance at A.A. meetings is basic of course. But reading, discussion with the counselor and others, lectures and seminars also are helpful.

2. **To help clients restructure their perception both of self and of environment.** The focus of this effort would be to help alcoholics see that

their sense of victimization is a function of their own thinking and doing. The author has found that many of his clients are surprised to learn that this feeling is virtually universal among alcoholics.

3. **To help clients structure their life so they may learn to find reward in sharing and giving.** In his own counseling the author has usually found this goal the first one achieved. For whatever reason alcoholics almost instinctively seem to find that their future health and well-being lies in giving to others by sharing their own experience. Much complementary support to achieve this goal comes from Alcoholics Anonymous. The idea is the premise upon which A.A. is structured.

4. **To help clients gain insight into those defenses which keep them persevering in their "stinkin thinkin."** Most often these include denial, rationalization, projection, and intellectualization.

5. **To help clients to elevate their self-esteem by helping them to see that failure is part of the human experience.** Just as important here is to help clients structure their lives for experiences, vocational, interpersonal where there is a high probability of success. The cornerstone of the client's self-esteem is continued sobriety and the counselor should bear in mind that the alcoholic client constantly is beset by the anxiety of a relapse.

**Periodic Reevaluation of Sobriety**

The best way to deal with this anxiety is to help the client discuss feelings and symptoms indicative of the alcoholic's latent but constant emotional menesis, the phenomenon termed *BUD,* building up to drink. These discussions must be interspersed and concurrent with the pursuit of secondary goals if the primary goal is to be achieved and maintained. The symptoms of BUD often come in combination and are as follows:

- Periods of silence in the usually talkative and cheerful client.
- Machine-gun like monologues by the client who usually speaks deliberately, slowly, quietly.
- Uncharacteristic irritability and/or hypomanic-like movements and activity.
- Unexplainable, acute fatigue.

- Listless, apathetic behavior in the usually active person.

- Focus and perseverance on depressed talk.

- Euphoric-like over confidence in the client's talk about how he/she will adhere to his/her sobriety.

If the client is unwilling to admit or to discuss these symptoms when the counselor sees them, the client invariably lapses into drink. What this counselor has observed is that symptoms usually become even stronger after the alcoholic begins drinking. In most cases however the lapse can be obviated if the client is helped to discuss symptoms both those apparent to the counselor and those felt by the client.

The reader might want to complement his/her reading of this section with a rereading of the section entitled ALCOHOLISM—THE RELAPSE which is in Part I of this book.

**Two Illustrations of Goal Setting**

The following two illustrations exemplify two approaches to counseling of the alcoholic. The first is termed *directivist,* the second *nondirectivist.* Both counselors are vitally concerned with the client's achievement of sobriety and both leave the responsibility of attaining it to the client but there the similarity ends.

The directivist is assertive, confrontative, at times harsh, and quickly responsive to the client's rationalizations and denials. At times he/she seems even harsh in his/her attack upon those defenses.

The nondirectivist is reserved. He/she does not give advice, believes rather the client should decide upon his/her own way. The counselor approach is to help the client come to his/her own realizations about the nature of his/her distorted perception and the futility of his/her "stinkin thinkin." The counselor focus is on developing a healthful positive relationship. Subsequent illustrations will include both approaches. The reader will decide for himself/herself which approach is more effective and may decide to incorporate aspects of each into his/her own counseling.

**Directivist.**

CO—Counselor CL—Client

CO *Ah, John good to see you come in, come in and sit.*

CL *Thanks. I'm sorry I'm late.*

CO *You were the first time we met too. You're nervous about seeing me?*

CL *Maybe a little.*

CO *Yeah, I appreciate that, but being late doesn't make me go away. You still want to see me right?*

CL *I guess.*

CO (Chuckles) *Not sure, eh?*

CL *I want to see you.*

CO *I know I'm not exactly loveable. I'm abrasive even. But I'm here John—all the time—and my job is just one, to help you stay sober. You want to stay sober?*

CL *I wouldn't be here if I didn't.*

CO (Nods) *Saying it's good. Important even. But if you were on time, maybe a little early even that would show me you really mean it.*

CL *I got held up at breakfast.*

CO *That's cause you were late there. You were coming in when I was going out. John, let's not bluff each other. Like I said yesterday, all the cards on the table. Otherwise my friend all we're going to do is shovel seaweed against the tide. I don't like to shovel. I got a bad back. Did you go to A.A. last night?*

CL *Yeah.*

CO *How much did you read of the book I gave you?*

CL *About a hundred pages.*

CO (Smiles) *That's good man.* (The counselor asks him questions about the reading.)

CL *How come all these questions. Don't you trust me?*

CO *I don't know you yet. Once you start opening up I'll know better how much I can trust you. Actually it doesn't matter if I trust you or not. What matters is that you trust yourself to do all the things you have to do to stay sober, A.A., the readings, opening up to me, and working on the weekends like you're supposed to.* (Counselor chuckles) *Yeah, and it would help if you trusted me.*

CL *Why are you badgering me?*

CO *I prefer to call it bird-dogging. I'm gonna bird-dog you til you don't need me.*

CL *I don't know how that's gonna help me. That's been my problem all my life, my boss, my wife, everybody badgers me—in fact everybody shits on me.*

CO *If they shit on you it's cause you let them. People treat you the way you let them. It's up to you how they treat you.*

What we saw in this brief excerpt is a hard-nosed counselor who makes it clear to the client what his goal responsibilities are and will be with respect to meeting time, A.A. attendance, reading, and self-disclosure.

**Nondirectivist.**

CO *Ah, Tom good to see you.*

CL *Sorry I'm late.*

CO *Only a few minutes. It happens. These first few sessions make most new people a little anxious.*

CL (Nods) *I know.*

CO *So what do you want to talk . . .*

CL *I went to the meeting. I really enjoyed it. Listening to that speaker made me realize a lot.*

CO *Tell me.*

CL *Well for one thing. I've really been a bastard to a lot of people for a long time.*

CO *Haven't we all?*

CL *What do you mean?*

CO *Just that all of us from time to time are selfish, petty, we lie, cheat. Those aren't sins peculiar to you.*

CL *No?*

CO *No. What matters is where we go from here. The past Tom, is a cancelled check. What matters is the future.*

CL *I don't see too much of a future, I don't even have a job anymore.*

CO *You'll get one.*

CL *I know but will I be able to keep it?*

CO *I honestly don't know that. Only you do. Only you can determine that.*

CL *That scares me. I just don't have any faith in myself for anything, leave alone getting and keeping a job. I mean what am I going to tell them when I apply, that I'm a drunk?*

CO *You don't want to tell them you're a drunk?*

CL *Christ no!*

CO *Hmm.*

CL (Laughs) *But I have to, huh?*

CO *Your decision.*

CL *How do you tell somebody you're a drunk?*

CO *Didn't the speaker do just that last night?*

CL *Yeah but that was A.A.*

CO *In front of what, forty, fifty people?*

CL *Yeah I get your drift. If he can do it with so many why can't I with one.*

CO *You already have. You told me.*

CL *You knew about me.*

CO *But this is the first time you actually said it.*

CL *This is different, you're supposed to understand. It's your job. Besides you're an alcoholic yourself. How does it make you feel to tell people?*

CO (Laughs) *Honest. It makes me feel honest.*

CL *I never feel like that.*

CO *Well?*

CL *I should try it, huh?*

CO *Your choice.*

CL *Don't you ever give advice?*

CO (Shakes his head) *Not usually. Life's hard enough without living it according to somebody else's opinion.*

This counselor while he alludes to goals, gives minimal direction, preferring to let the client carry the counseling ball. His focus, if you examine the excerpt, is the relationship and letting the client choose his own way.

# RAPPORT

## Definition, Research, and Discussion

As in the French from which it is borrowed *rapport,* in general, has to do with accord and affinity in a relationship. In *counseling rapport means that there is warmth and trust between the counseling participants, an emotional give and take critical to counseling.* Two researchers found that its establishment inevitably facilitates the resolution of interpersonal problems and at least one study concluded that if rapport cannot be established, the client should be referred (Cheng & Hsin, 1973; Katsuhiko, 1969).

Qualities which make for an effective therapist, explained in Part II of this book, facilitate the establishment of rapport. Briefly, those included an optimistic perception, authenticity, acceptance, nurturance, and compassion. Axelson (1967) found that the counselor quality which establishes rapport most quickly and effectively is an *empathic disposition.* Although the word empathy has been used in other contexts a number of times, perhaps taking a closer look at it might be profitable because of its close relationship to rapport. Empathy is derived from the German Einfuhlung which means "feeling into." One of the more complete explanations of the meaning of empathy in counseling was given by Arnold Bucheimer (1961) in an address to the American Personnel and Guidance Association (now American Association of Counseling and Development). In this address he described five aspects of empathy:

1. **Tone,** which has to do with harmony and mutuality with which the counselor and client interact.

2. **Pace,** which has to do with the timing with which the counselor leads the client.

3. **Flexibility,** which has to do with the counselor's ability to adapt to new climatic moments and ignore and discard previously thought out procedures.

4. **Frame of reference,** which has to do with becoming attuned to and gaining an understanding from where the client is coming

and then rephrasing, reflecting, and getting at the essence of what the client is communicating.

5. **Repertoire of leads,** which has to do with the counselor's ability to respond to both verbal and nonverbal contexts of the client's content.

One can rightly conclude from Bucheimer's (1961) thoughts then that the counselor's ability to establish rapport is closely allied to his/her ability to empathize effectively.

When the client comes for the initial contact, the emotional climate may be strained. This strain is understandable. The client is meeting a stranger with whom he/she is obligated to share thoughts and feelings which until that moment have been viewed as supremely private. Add to that all the characteristics associated with the alcoholic personality as outlined in Part I of this book and it becomes transparently clear why the initial moments might be strained. The counselor then has the obligation to relax and relieve the initial strained moments. Some counselors believe that the best approach is to open with a neutral topic like the weather. Others believe that the neutral topic approach is a waste. Counseling finally is not a social chit-chat. Moreover chit-chat sometimes leads to even more tension if the counselor has not developed a more communicative approach. In his/her opening remarks the counselor should focus on why the client is in his/her office. After the initial greetings and amenities the counselor may make these kinds of comments, *"I'm glad you're here, tell me how I can help." "I'm your counselor. This is your hour." "The fact that you're here tells me that you want to start back to something better."*

More often than not the counselor has access to client records regarding background and family. These data should be examined before the first session so that the counselor can ask open-ended questions. Questions about work usually are appropriate, i.e., *"I understand you're a cop. Tell me what is it like?" "I understand you were just promoted to foreman. How is it different from being on the line?" "You're a teacher, I understand. What's it like?"* When delivered with a casual appropriate tone, comments and questions such as these facilitate communication. They are meaningful questions to the client because they are about him/her and unlike social chit-chat they are forthright because they focus on the reality of the client's presence.

At the same time recognize clearly that rapport is more than just relaxing a client and getting underway. It transcends the whole process of counseling. It is constant. It continues from initial contact to termination and is characterized by cordiality, confidence, and cooperation. It is a working relationship but it is more too. Rapport in counseling inevitably develops into a relationship between counselor and client which is unique, far different from most other relationships that the client has.

The author asked a directivist and a nondirectivist to express their views on the subject of rapport. Both responses were taperecorded.

### Directivist Views of Rapport

**Male, Forty-one Years Old, Eleven Years an Alcoholism Counselor, Ed.M. in Counseling, and a Recovering Alcoholic.**

> *What can I tell ya? I think rapport's important. Course it's important. Who could say otherwise? But to be honest with ya' I don't myself focus on it. I focus on the purpose, the goal—sobriety. Rapport has to do with being liked. To be frank with you, I don't care whether my patients like me or not. I'm not running in any beauty contest. There's one issue and one only—the patient's sobriety.*
>
> *When a patient comes to me that first day I tell him plain and simple, "I'm not your nurse maid, I'm not even sure I'm your friend. I don't know you yet.* ***I am your counselor.*** *I'll help by listening and if asked, I'll answer straight forward. I expect the same." I don't like patients who make like they're Spanish athletes, ya' know, throw the bull. Only one way a patient can make progress and that's if he's completely honest, right to where it hurts him/her and hurts badly. Before my patient can do that I gotta do the same thing. So I do it. I tell him and if it's a her I tell her too, about me and booze. By the time I'm through, takes about three sessions, I usually have my rapport. At least they know me. And that's where it's at in this game. If you want rapport, patients have gotta feel they know you, before they can trust you. And in this business trust is where it's all at. Once patients trust you, they will let you take the first step with them down that awful long road back to life.*

## Nondirectivist Views of Rapport

**Female, Thirty-two Years Old, Six Years a Counselor, the Last Three with Alcoholics, M.A. in Clinical Psychology.**

> *Rapport is critical. It is the foundation of the whole process. Without it you have no counseling, you can't because you have no trust. Prior to my coming here I worked with mentally handicapped, retarded children. Rapport was so easy there. They loved me immediately. It's very difficult here. The nature of the problem makes it so. Alcoholics are paranoid to begin with. Their defenses revolve around projection. I've noticed that it's especially bad when they're coming off the booze. Somebody really should do a study to see what the relationship is between guilt and projection. That's what I find in my first contact—guilt and projection. I suspect that's why I find obtaining rapport difficult. It takes me several sessions to begin to feel we have it. I could do like most of my colleagues and confront, confront, confront, but I won't. My training and my convictions are that all clients, even alcoholics, have the capacity to help and to heal themselves to the extent they can and to which they want. Confrontation does not hurry that process I don't think. Anyway, my way toward rapport and toward help of the alcoholic might be a little slower but I think it's sounder.*

## Obstacles to Establishment of Rapport

Some obstacles effectively can block the establishment of rapport. These include

- a lack in counselor ego strength,
- unmotivated client,
- client's negative perception of counselor, and
- personality clash.

**Counselor Ego Strength.** Deficiencies in the counselor's ego can interfere with the establishment of rapport. In counseling he/she does need to have an ego which is strong—strong enough to focus, attend, and adhere to the client. The counselor should be disciplined enough to prevent and block irrelevant and distracting thoughts from interfering with the ability to meet needs of clients. In short when doing therapy, the counselor should be able to keep personal life compartmentalized and the healthful ego should be in total control of his/her personality.

**Unmotivated Client.** Sometimes the counselor finds himself/herself with a client who geuninely is not motivated, a client who has not "bottomed out," but who is at best conflicted in his/her own self-referral, or worse who has been mandated into therapy, a not uncommon phenomenon especially with recent drinking and driving legislation.

To establish a meaningful productive rapport under a mandated referral is especially difficult if not impossible. The length of time for counseling usually is fixed and the client, of course, knows it. More often than not, such clients present themselves as victims. Not uncommonly they are resentful, hostile, and sometimes do not even try to hide their boredom. At best such clients attempt to manipulate the counselor by putting on a deferential, even submissive manner so that they can fulfill their obligations, "serve their time," and get the note for the judge which will let them drive—and drink again. Counseling under these conditions is an exercise in futility.

**Client's Negative Perception of Counselor.** Rapport establishment is often difficult when the client perceives the counselor negatively. This negative perception usually has nothing to do with the counselor's competencies or credentials but has to do with the needs and perception of the client. For example, the counselor may be years, decades, even a generation younger than the client. Under such circumstances the client's view might be *" What can a counselor who's young enough to be my son/daughter do for me?"* or again the client may be well aware of the fact that there are counselors available who are themselves recovering alcoholics. Such clients are convinced that their nonalcoholic counselor can't help them. The competent, knowledgeable counselor must learn to take such situations in stride. Even so, the recommendation is that, if possible the counselor should hold several sessions with the client, assess the situation, and, if in good conscience he/she feels that meaningful rapport has not been established, then the client should be referred to another counselor.

**Personality Clash.** Sometimes rapport cannot be established because of a personality clash. For the counselor this should be a very rare occurrence indeed. The truth is however that counselors also have their own idiosyncratic dynamics. As a result each counselor will find he/she has difficulty in working with some clients for whatever reasons. Even so the counselor should be perceptive and honest enough to know the potential for an ineffective relationship by the end of the first session, certainly no later than the second, and then after discussing the problems honestly and kindly, the client should be referred. To delay the referral will result in communication of a personal rejection later—something no alcoholic needs. Just as bad, it may result in little or no progress in the counseling.

## SETTING

### Counseling Room

Research indicates that physical setting influences how people perceive each other. A study by Maslow and Mintz (1956) and another by Mintz (1956) alone showed that people perceive more optimistically when the room in which they are situated is attractive. Conversely they perceive more pessimistically when the room is shabby. These studies suggest that time, energy, and money should be invested in making the counseling room attractive and comfortable. Pictures and draperies should be hung, rugs laid, and flowers or plants added. The validity of such efforts is reflected in a study by Chaikin (1976) who found that the more positively a client perceives the room, the more positively he/she will relate to the counselor. In short, a room decorated with care can only enhance the counseling process.

Haase and DiMattia (1970) did a study to determine what kind of seating arrangements counselors and clients preferred most. The arrangement they found to be the most popular was the one which is used most, the client sitting at the side of the desk. Widgery and Stackpole (1972) found that the position of the desk influences the counselor's credibility. Those clients who were binding much anxiety rated counselor credibility higher when there was no desk. Those with low anxiety rated it higher when there was a desk.

### Space

The effect of space upon the counseling process also has been investigated. Haase and DiMattia (1976) have found that smaller rooms tend to inhibit the length and duration of self-reference talk. In another study Haase (1970) found that which sex a client is does not influence the distance preferred between counseling participants. Both males and females indicated that between 30 and 39 inches was about right. Research in social and familial settings indicate that this is the distance preferred by spouses and by intimate friends. It is interesting that clients feel that the same kind of distance is best for counseling.

## COMMUNICATION

Communication between counselor and client is the essence of the counseling experience. Without it there is no counseling.

Because communication is so essential in counseling Satir (1975) observed how her clients communicate and in so doing gained a better understanding of what was being communicated than words alone may tell. She has noted that clients communicate in five ways. These are placating, blaming, super-reasonable, irrelevant, and congruent.

The person who relates by *placating* is the one who is outwardly agreeable even when his/her feelings are really the opposite. This is not an uncommon way of behaving for many alcoholics. The distance between what they feel and what they show, keeps them disgruntled, angry, and more often than not unattuned to what's going on around them.

The *blaming* person is usually one who perceives threat everywhere. Blamers come in many forms and styles, i.e., they nag, they're constantly expressing dissatisfaction, they rant and rage, they usually belittle the successes of others. The blamer is a person who is always looking out, never in. To the blamer life is usually all about luck—good luck and bad luck. The alcoholic's own life is viewed as luckless. Important to the blamer is the idea that you really can't trust anyone. Everyone is viewed as having a little bag and is selling something. For many alcoholics this cynical view of people provides the excellent rationalization to continue to drink.

The *super-reasonable* person more often than not is a guilt-ridden individual who has surrendered to his/her environment. This is especially true of female alcoholics. Such persons suffer from an acutely low self-esteem. Their constant conciliatory stance can be understood as a response to their lack of self-esteem. Basically they don't feel they have much to offer or any convictions worth defending, even holding. Compounding the problem is their terror that they will finally be left alone. And so they present themselves to others much like dependent children. Such a way of relating ironically diminishes their already low self-esteem. What should be noted about this super-reasonable type is that beneath the thick veneer of dependency beats a very angry heart, all of which of course is denied.

This author has observed that many alcoholics have a remarkable penchant for the *irrelevant.* The reasons are the usual ones for alcoholics: fear of the unknown, fear of their own emotions, mistrust of the counselor, and an honest ignorance of what their emotions actually are. And so clients discuss topics, people, situations, events which have little to do with their lives and especially with their drinking.

*Congruent* communication is found in the client who is recovering. This person is able to express and examine his/her true feelings. The counselor is able to tell when this client is on the road to recovery because in counseling the words, tones, and general behavior all gibe. The perceptive counselor invariably has good feelings about the recovering client and sessions spent with him/her.

### Via Body and Emotions

DeRivera (1977) is one who believes that emotions and body are very much woven together. His work has led him to conclude that emotions ". . . both influence the body and reflect the condition of the body." This view is comparable to one expressed earlier by the noted psychiatrist Thomas Szasz (1961) when he wrote that most of our bodily symptoms are no more than "cries for help." The alcoholic who when sober, is too often perspiring profusely, who is constantly complaining of headaches and a variety of ailments may be saying only, *"Help me, I'm in trouble. I want to talk about me."* Unfortunately, what he/she wants to talk about are physical ailments. But what should be noted is that these ailments can indeed be a starting point for what should be the focus—the emotional dysfunctions which have precipitated the client's addiction.

Communication occurs in a variety of ways, with words, with tones, with behaviors. When these are congruent, the message is simple, clear, and direct. Communication becomes garbled, however, when words, tones, and emotions do not gibe and they do not often with many alcoholic clients. *"Damn it, I'm not mad,"* spits out the client; or again, *"No I wasn't hurt, at least not that much, when he called me a drunken slob,"* she says wiping her eyes.

**Levels of Communication**

Human communication is too often complicated. Communication becomes especially intriguing when it occurs on different levels, the unconscious as well as the conscious. Freud (1959) was the first who pointed out this phenomenon. He explained in a convincing way that at times people let their ego relax, give vent to id strivings, and via the verbal slip, memory loss, or behavior let their true feelings come forth. Such emissions are unconscious but should be taken seriously as they have the greatest meaning. Thus he wrote, "the slip itself makes sense" and should be viewed "as a valid mental process following out its own purpose."

That human beings have to resort to unconscious messages is of course a sad commentary upon human interaction. That they do so, however, reflects the frustration, intense need, and determination which all people have to reach out, express themselves, in a word communicate. Nowhere is this seen better than in the alcoholic. Most alcoholics feel that their messages are not received, that no one is listening, that no one even cares to listen—ergo the alcoholism. *Their alcoholism can quite rightly be understood as a message, a message that they have given up, surrendered to a cruel environment.*

**Via Double Messages**

The confusion and fear which alcoholics experience in trying to communicate are due in no small part to the lack of learning and mislearning they underwent during the critical childhood years. Many of them never learned how to communicate in a congruent fashion (words, tones, behavior gibed) because they weren't exposed to such communications within their families. They were exposed rather to double messages,i.e., *"Of course I love you darling and you know how much I do too. But I'm really, really sorry I just can't come to the play this morning. It's that awful migraine again. I'll make it next time. Promise. Come, give mother a big kiss. Hurry now, or you'll be late for school."* Messages such as these have a devastating effect upon a child. They split him/her in two emotionally. Which message does the child accept? Desperately he/she wants to believe and accept the words of love punctuated with a kiss. Yet there's the other message there too, a message of rejection brutally exemplified in an absent mother with the perennial migraine. And the conflict for the child necessarily becomes more acute especially when the child begins to learn that gin is simply not an appropriate medicine for a migraine. The conflict and confusion inevitably result in a latent, constant depression when the child begins to *feel* (children simply don't intellectualize) that mother loves booze more than him/her. In any case the home where a pattern of double messages is the communicative style is a home which breeds confused and too often uncommunicative people.

### Via Body Language

The body is a prime vehicle for communication. How a client takes *care of it, spaces it,* and *uses it* tells the counselor much about the client.

The client who comes in looking impeccably well groomed simply does not have the same self-view of the world as one who comes in smelling and looking like he/she needs a bath. Quite apparently the former communicates a strong concern for self, perhaps for counseling. Conversely the latter person is on the skids and doesn't care. Self-care is a reflection of self-love and self-esteem and is demonstrated physically in one's appearance.

This author has found useful to have at least a couple of alternative chairs available for the client. Where the client sits in relation to the counselor also reflects something about his/her interest and motivation to communicate. Accordingly, this counselor makes it a point to sit in his chair first and lets the client choose his/her seat, one being farther away from the counselor (about five feet) than the other (about three feet). That distance a client sits from the counselor affects process is supported in research data. Knight and Blair (1976) for example, found that the distance between counselor and client affects client comfort. Stone and Morden (1976) found that when clients sat too close or too far from the counselor, they were more inhibited about their self-disclosures than if they sat at an intermediate distance.

The language of body motion has been the topic for research and discussion now for almost two decades (Ekman & Friesen, 1969; Kendon, 1972), and quite rightly so. By and large a relaxed person sits casually. In the protected, emotionally charged climate of counseling *most clients display their feelings via their bodies,* on their faces usually, or with a leg that swings, a hand that drums, or a general shifting and reshifting of their bodies. Even the immobile, stone-faced clients are telling the counselor something—they are hide-bound by their denial and/or intellectualization defenses. In sum, the perceptive counselor is one who is sensitive to the body movements of his/her clients. And, if appropriate, will react and deal with them.

### Via Defenses

The clinical roots of communication are found in psychological defense. Another way to understand the communication system of the alcoholic then, is to approach it via his/her defense system. The most salient defense in the alcoholic's repertoire is denial. Rationalization, intellectualization, and projection are used too, usually to support denial.

**Denial.** The refusal to acknowledge one's behavior and effects of it upon oneself and others invariably engenders guilt. Not uncommonly the guilt effects changes in the alcoholic's personality, i.e., submissiveness, passivity, or again the guilt may precipitate behaviors at the other end of the behavioral continuum—fits of anger, temper tantrum. One of the more insidious aspects of denial is that too often it seems to infect others close to the alcoholic. They too begin to deny. They joke about the alcoholic's drinking, tolerate it, even protect him/her in it. Not uncommonly, after a time they begin to see the drunkenness as part of the general personality. Communication, if at all, focuses on irrelevancies. Any occasional attempt by a friend or family member to confront or even broach the subject of drink seems futile. Compounding the problem further is the fact that often the alcoholic becomes positively creative in thwarting such attempts. This response to what is perceived as an attack upon his/her denial may be a humorous quip, indifference, anger, or worst of all, a stoney silence.

**Rationalization.** Communication with rationalizers is almost impossible. They neatly justify what they do, say, even what they themselves think. Rationalization is an important prop for denial. Alcoholic rationalizations are all too familiar. *"I only drink beer, never the hard stuff." "I never drink before noontime"* or again, *"Only on weekends," "I just don't drink that much, a pint of gin a day just isn't that much, besides I haven't missed a day's work in almost two months."*

**Intellectualization.** Often a prop for the alcoholic's denial is intellectualization. With the highly intelligent person intellectualization is especially difficult to break down. The reason for this difficulty is that the intellectualizer talks and seems to function as if he/she has no emotions. He/she behaves as if joy, rage, and despair are not part of his/her ken. This lack of emotion combined with a refined ability to think, reflect, and analyze makes any meaningful communication difficult.

The best way to deal with intellectualizing alcoholics is precisely *not* to intellectualize, not to duel with them intellectually, with logic, or with analyses. The weak link in their armor is emotion. They refuse to acknowledge their own emotion, and are more often than not befuddled if not terrified by the emotion exhibited by others. Thus, they belittle emotion, scorn it, or react indifferently to it, because they do not know how to deal with it. Accordingly, the counselor's responses should be inflected with feeling tones and all comments and questions should focus on the client's emotions. The following illustrations might prove helpful.

**Directivist—Illustrative Excerpt on Intellectualization.**

CO *Now let me get this straight, you mean to tell me that your wife had half of your pay legally attached and deposited in her account? She actually did that?*

CL *Yeah, she did that.*

CO *Wow!*

CL *Actually, I can understand her doing that.*

CO *Okay, you can understand it, but explain to me how did it make you feel? I mean in your gut. How did it make you feel?*

CL *Well to be honest, I'm not sure. What was important was what to do. I thought about it and I went to my lawyer.*

CO *John, weren't you angry, upset?*

**Nondirectivist—Illustrative Excerpt on Intellectualization.**

CO *You say your wife had your pay attached.*

CL *Yes.*

CO *How did that you make you feel?*

CL (Shrugs) *I'm not really sure. I did check with my lawyer. It was legally appropriate.*

CO *Did the legality assuage any possible feelings of anger you might have had?*

CL (Pause) *To be honest about it, I'm not sure.*

CO *You said your drinking increased dramatically after the attachment.*

CL *That's true.*

CO *And what might that tell you, John?*

Both counselors are following their convictions about the approach. The directivist is himself more emotional. The nondirectivist, it should be noted, gets into a little dueling with his client, manipulating him, almost trapping him into admitting he had to feel anger at the attachment. Both counselors however focus on the real issue, the intellectualizer's apparent alienation from his feelings about the matter.

**Projection.** Communication with alcoholics who project stretches a counselor's patience to the limit. The essence of the problem is that projectors perceive people as being basically hostile, or selfish, or unconcerned with them. People don't like them. (These feelings, of course, are ones which they harbor about themselves.) In any case what projecting alcoholics do is test people. They make demand upon demand until people react negatively thereby confirming alcoholic's basic perception that people don't like alcoholics.

In counseling, problems are considerable. As has been observed, the essential ingredient for counseling to proceed is rapport founded on trust. The projector finds this intolerably difficult. Testing of the counselor may take a variety of forms, i.e., late for appointment, self-disclosing little bombshells a few moments before the end of the hour to extend it, cynical comments about counseling, and so forth. The most effective way with this client is firmness and adherence to agreed upon ground rules. For example, if the client comes late, he/she gets only the balance of his scheduled hour, little bombshells are held over to the next hour, cynical comments are ignored. The counselor cannot permit manipulation by this type of client for a moment. Rapport will not be obtained that way for the obvious reason that trust cannot be obtained in a relationship where there is manipulation.

## TRANSFERENCE

### Definition

Briefly, the transference occurs because of two dynamic phenomena—repression and identification. The client who was exposed to parental rejection in childhood and/or was not permitted to express his/her true feelings toward parents represses these feelings. These repressions stultify emotional development and invariably result in problems in sexual identification.

In the emotionally sheltered climate of counseling the client who develops rapport with the counselor identifies with him/her and inevitably goes into transference; that is the client attaches feelings repressed in childhood toward the rejecting parent(s). The parent figure(s) and the therapist unconsciously blend for him, and they may do so even if the rejecting parent figure and the therapist are of different sexes.

The transference can be positive or it can be negative. Whichever it is is dependent upon the nature of childhood repression. Thus if in childhood the client was too terrified to express dissatisfaction or hostility, then in the transference (negative) the client will vent these feelings upon the therapist. If as a child the client was not able to attach feelings of love, then the transference is characterized by these kinds of feelings for the therapist.

By working through the transference with the counselor the client gains insight into the cause of the problem. The alcoholic gains insight into what his/her true feelings are about himself and others, the counselor included.

The reader should know that transference is a phenomenon dealt with by the psychoanalyst. Many, perhaps most counselors, do not deal with it as the lead-in to insight but treat it lightly, if at all. Three of the most renown among these are Carl Rogers, the exponent of client-centered therapy; Albert Ellis, the exponent of rational emotive therapy; and Joseph Wolpe, the advocate of conditioning therapy.

This author, who is not a psychoanalyst, tends to agree with Thorne (1950) (who is not an analyst either) that ". . . it is necessary for the counselor to understand its nature since it may be anticipated that such relationships tend to develop automatically if the counseling process reaches deep emotional levels of personality." Wolberg (1954) a renowned analyst, feels that transference is inevitable. "Sooner or later a patient will 'transfer' past attitudes and feelings into the present relationship."

**Manifestations**

Whatever one's position may be on the issue of transference, the author believes that the counselor who is oblivious of its nature will be at a disadvantage in dealing with his/her client. To obviate this disadvantage, some manifestations of transference are outlined.

**Positive Transference.**

1. The positive attitudes expressed by the client increase, i.e., *"I like you. I feel you really understand me,"* and so forth.

2. The client begins to ask questions about the counselor's personal life. *"Are you married? Are you from around here?"* and so forth.

3. The client begins to sit closer.

4. The client may seek to touch the counselor.

5. The client who initially arrived a little late for appointments begins to show up promptly, even early.

**Negative Transference.**

1. The client begins to express negative attitudes, if not about the counselor, then about counseling, i.e., *"I think this is really a lot of crap. I'm not sure you're helping me. Did you really have to go to school for this?"*

2. The client begins to sit farther away.

3. The client, initially talkative, may fall into protracted periods of silence.

4. The client begins to arrive late, may even begin to cancel appointments.

## Treatment

The alcoholism counselor has a variety of options.

1. The counselor may, as many do, simply ignore the dynamics of the transference and focus on the alcoholic's behaviors.

2. The counselor may focus on those aspects of the transference which seem especially pertinent to the client's life now or which threaten to thwart progress already made. For example, if the client is of the opposite sex and feels he/she is in love with the counselor, the counselor may feel that an explanation of the dynamics might be in order. This author feels that such an explanation would be prudent. Without such an explanation a client could interpret the counselor's responses as being cool, uninterested, and essentially rejecting. Interpretations such as these would probably terminate the counseling at a critical juncture.

3. The counselor could pursue an analytic approach seeking to work through the transference by probing with questions focusing on the client's childhood.

# COUNTERTRANSFERENCE

## Definition

A countertransference occurs when the counselor attaches repressed feelings to the client. (See discussion under Professional Qualities, Part II). However, it should be pointed out that the counselor can effectively prevent a full blown countertransference if he/she is acutely sensitive to all of its symptoms.

## Symptoms—Positive

The obvious positive symptoms are that the counselor is attracted sexually to the physical aspects of the client, obsessed in off-hours about the client, looking forward to sessions with the client, spending more time in physical grooming for the sessions than typical, and so forth.

During sessions the counselor finds that he/she is probing into aspects of the client's life and habits which are at best only tangentially related to the alcoholism problem.

The counselor does for the client what he/she ordinarily does not do with others, i.e., helps the client on and off with coat, offers coffee, brings in donuts, and so forth.

The symptoms of a positive countertransference are transparent. The reader should know that too often they are not so to the counselor who is suffering it. The ethical, competent counselor suffers it indeed. Less than a year ago this author received a call late on a Friday night from a colleague, a 37 year old single woman with a flawless reputation for both competence and ethics, who counsels in a local clinic. She was very distraught and wanted to talk. She came to this author's home and told him how she had agreed to a date for the next night with a 45 year old divorced client who was in her professional judgement a recovered alcoholic. She had had five sessions with him once a week for the past five weeks. The woman, who dated seldom and who could fairly be described as "average looking," when queried about the client described him as a handsome and once successful lawyer who was practicing again. When asked why she had come to talk she replied embarrassedly that she wanted confirmation that the date she'd made was okay, wasn't it? The author who felt pompous even sanctimonious doing it, told her he felt it was inappropriate, even unethical, and that she was in a classic countertransference. She left, kept the date, went through a stormy love affair with him, which terminated recently. She is still a practicing counselor. The lawyer is still sober and still single.

What the reader should conclude from this is that a countertransference can happen to the very best of counselors. No guaranteed way can be given to prevent one. The best, the only prescription to minimize its happening, is for the counselor to know what his/her weaknesses are with respect to other human beings.

**Symptoms—Negative**

The symptoms of a negative countertransference are easy to detect but even more easily rationalized.

The obvious negative symptoms are that the counselor is irritated by client's speech, manner, dress, and so forth. Also the counselor finds that he/she is discussing the client with colleagues in a disparaging way, dreads sessions with the client, is uninterested, inattentive, and bored during the sessions.

The counselor forgets an appointment, cuts it short, even cancels appointments.

Progress is slow, if at all.

A negative contertransference can happen but it should happen very rarely. Again, the best prescription for its prevention is a strong counselor sense of self-awareness.

## INSIGHT

Many counseling theorists believe that achievement of insight is an indispensable requisite to the whole counseling process. According to Munroe (1955) "the crux of the therapeutic process is the development of insight." Wolberg (1954) believed that insight is basic to counseling despite school or approach, "Insight on some level is fundamental in all therapies." Sustained change toward a more healthful life, these therapists argue, is not possible without insight achievement. There are counselors who disagree with this view. Skinner (1956) in one paper and Hobbs (1962) in a later one have both questioned the importance and significance of insight in bringing about change.

### Definition

What exactly is insight? This author defines it as *an intellectual understanding and an emotional appreciation of the why of the problem(s) which led the client to seek counseling. Both* the intellectual and emotional levels of appreciation are critical. An intellectual understanding without concomitant feelings is simply not enough. This counselor has sat many times with alcoholic clients who explained, analyzed, and interpreted the why of their own behavior. They sounded positively insightful doing so. Then they went out and got drunk. Intellectual understanding is not enough.

### Importance of Insight

When both an intellectual understanding and an emotional appreciation about the *why* of drinking exist, the question remains, can a guarantee be given that the alcoholic will achieve his/her sobriety? The answer is no. Guarantees as one wag put it are found on boxes of soap powders. There simply are none in human dynamics. This too, must be said, however, that while the client may not stop drinking because he/she has achieved insight, he/she definitely will not stop drinking if he/she has not achieved it. In short, the counselor can conclude that helping a client to achieve insight has merit.

## TERMINATION

### Uniqueness of Alcoholism Termination

Ordinarily the counseling process has a period of time devoted to termination. This period is considered important by most counselors as it prepares the client to integrate what he/she has learned about himself/herself, to rid the self of any vestiges of dependency, and to prevent any depression over the sense of loss about ending a unique relationship. Commonly, termination generates a measure of anxiety in the client.

None of these termination activities need be true in counseling the alcoholic. The author's conviction is that **formal termination in alcoholism counseling is inappropriate.** Even when a prolonged and healthful state of sobriety has been reached, the door should be left open for subsequent contact. No alcoholic is ever cured of the anxiety associated with taking a drink. It is this knowledge which has led this counselor to do what he never does with clients suffering from other types of illness. He calls his alcoholic clients periodically to learn how they are doing. More than a few times these calls have resulted in added counseling sessions. The latent anxiety this counselor feels about terminating his clients is shared by other counselors. Goodyear (1981) in a recent provocative paper observed that termination is a loss experience for the counselor as well as the client. Counselors, he pointed out, often have anxieties about client competence and may suffer feelings of guilt and sadness when their clients are leaving. This counselor has experienced these feelings about his clients generally and about his alcoholic clients in particular.

## SUMMARY

· Among alcoholics there exist phenomena termed high, low, and middle bottom. Each alcoholic arrives at his/her bottom differently and for different reasons. The level and nature of the bottom varies with the person and always embraces the alcoholic's entire dynamic system. Meaningful, effective counseling can occur only when the alcoholic experiences his/her private bottom.

Goals are basic issues in counseling. The primary goal in counseling the alcoholic is the achievement of *continuing sobriety.* The secondary goals are important too, as they facilitate the achievement of the primary goal. Periodic reevaluation of the client's sobriety is critical if it is to be maintained because most alcoholics experience the BUD phenomenon.

Rapport has to do with accord, affinity, warmth, and trust in a relationship. Tone, pace, flexibility, frame of reference, and repertoire of leads are all integral aspects of rapport. Rapport transcends the whole process of counseling. Counselor ego strength, an unmotivated client, a client's negative perception of his/her counselor, and a clash in personalities are all potential obstacles to the development of rapport.

The setting in which counseling is done can affect it. The size of the room and the seating arrangements bear important consideration. Time, energy, and money should be invested in making the counseling room attractive.

Communication between counselor and client is the essence of the counseling experience. Placating, blaming, super-reasonableness, irrelevance, and congruence are five ways of communicating. Clients communicate also via body and emotion, on unconscious levels, via double message with body language and via defenses.

Transference is a function of repression and identification. The transference can manifest itself both positively and negatively. The counselor can ignore it, focus on those aspects which are pertinent to the client's life, or can pursue an analytic approach.

As is the case with transference, countertransference has both positive and negative symptoms. The best prescription for minimizing the occurrence of a positive or negative countertransference is for the counselor to have a full appreciation of self.

Some believe that achievement of insight is an indispensable requisite to the counseling process. Achievement of insight by the alcoholic as to the why of his/her addiction is no guarantee that sobriety will be achieved, but the alcoholic will definitely not stop drinking if insight is not achieved.

Formal termination in alcoholism counseling is inappropriate because alcoholics live with a constant latent anxiety that they will relapse into drink. Accordingly, periodic check-ups by counselors of their clients is appropriate.

## TOPICS FOR DISCUSSION AND REFLECTION

1. Why are some bottoms reached quickly (a matter of months) and some never?

2. Articulate what are for you the primary goals for your professional counseling.

3. Which approach has more merit for you—the directivist or the non-directivist approach? Why?

4. What personal and professional qualities do you harbor which will facilitate and/or hinder rapport with clients?

5. What body language habits do you possess which facilitate and/or hinder communication with clients?

6. What needs do you have which may be conducive to a counter-transference?

7. How can counselor awareness and sensitivity to the transference phenomena help the client? The counselor?

8. What is your definition and/or criteria for achievement of client insight?

# BIBLIOGRAPHY


Axelson, J. A. (1967). The relationship of counselor candidates empathic perception and rapport in small group interaction. *Counselor Education and Supervision, 6*(4), 287-292.

Boy, A. V., & Pine, G. J. (1976). Equalizing the counseling relationship: Psychotherapy. *Theory, Research, and Practice, 13* (1), 20-25.

Bucheimer, A. (March 28, 1961). Empathy in counseling paper delivered at *A.P.G.A.* convention.

Chaikin, A. L., Derlega, V. J., & Miller, S. J. (1976). Effects of room environment on self-disclosure in a counseling analogue. *Journal of Counseling Psychology, 23* (5),479-481.

Cheng, A., & Hsin, H. (1973). Rapport in initial counseling interview and its impact in effectiveness. *Acta Psychologica Taiwanica, 15,* 31-40.

DeRivera, J. (1977). A structural theory of the emotions. *Psychological Issues, 10* (4), 34.

Ekman, P., & Friesen, W. V. (1969). Non-verbal leakage and clues to deception. *Psychiatry, 32,* 88-105.

Freud, S. (1949). *A General Introduction to Psychoanalysis.* New York: Perma Giants.

Freud, S. (1959). The dynamics of the transference. In S. Freud, *The Collected Papers,* Vol. II. New York: Basic Books.

Goodyear, R. K. (1981). Termination as a loss experience for the counselor. *The Personnel and Guidance Journal, 59* (6), 347-350.

Haase, R. F. (1970). The relationship of sex and instructional set to the regulation of interpersonal interaction distance in a counseling analogue. *Journal of Counseling Psychology, 17* (5), 233-236.

Haase, R. F., & DiMattia, D. J. (1976). Spatial environments and verbal conditioning in a quasi-counseling interview. *Journal of Counseling Psychology, 23* (5), 414-421.

Haase, R. F., & DiMattia, D. J. (1970). Proxemic behavior: Counselor, administrator, and client preference for seating arrangements in dyadic interaction. *Journal of Counseling Psychology, 17* (7), 319-325.

Hobbs, N. (1962). Sources of gain in psychotherapy. *American Psychology, 17,* 741-747.

Kanner, L. (1963). The scope and goal of psychotherapy with children. *American Journal of Psychotherapy, 17,* 366-374.

Katsuhiko, S. (1969). An analysis of the change in rapport during counseling. *Japanese Journal of Child Psychiatry, 10* (3), 180-188.

Kendon, A. (1972). How people interact. In A. Ferber, M. Mendelsohn & A. Napier (Eds.), *The Book of Family Therapy,* Science House: New York.

Knight, P. H., & Blair, C. K. (1976). Degree of client comfort as a function of dyadic interaction distance. *Journal of Counseling Psychology, 23* (1), 13-16.

Maslow, A. H., & Mintz, N. (1956). Effects of esthetic surroundings: Initial short-term effects of three esthetic conditions upon perceiving "energy" and well being in faces. *Journal of Counseling Psychology, 41,* 247-254.

Mintz, W. L. (1956). Effects of esthetic surroundings: Prolonged and repeated experience in a "beautiful" and ugly room. *Journal of Psychology, 41,* 459-466.

Munroe, R. (1955). *Schools of Psychoanalytic Thought.* New York: Henry Holt.

Patterson, C. H. (1963). Control, conditioning, and counseling. *The Personnel and Guidance Journal, 41,* 680-686.

Pepinsky, H. B., & Karst, T. O. (1964). Convergence: A phenomenon in counseling and psychotherapy. *American Psychologist, 19,* 333-338.

Rogers, C. R. (1961). The place of the person in the new world of the behavioral sciences. *The Personnel and Guidance Journal, 39* (6), 442-451.

Rudikoff, L. C., & Kirk, B. A. (1961). Goals of counseling: Mobilizing the counselee. *Journal of Counseling Psychology, 8,* 243-249.

Satir, V. (1975). You as a change agent in helping families to change. In V. Satir, J. Stachowiak, & H. Taskman (Eds.), *Helping Families to Change* (p. 41). New York: Jason Bronson.

Skinner, B. F. (1956). Critique of psychoanalytic concepts and theories. In H. Feigl & M. Scrivin (Eds.), *Minnesota Studies in the Philosophy of Science* (p. 85). Minneapolis: University of Minnesota Press.

Stone, G., & Morden, C. (1976). Effect of distance on verbal productivity. *Journal of Counseling Psychology, 23* (5), 486-488.

Szasz, T. S. (1961). *The Myth of Mental Illness.* New York: Harper and Roe.

Thorne, F. C. (1950). Principles of personality counseling: An eclectic viewpoint. *Journal of Clinical Psychology,* 233.

Widgery, R., & Stackpole, C. (1972). Desk position, interviewer anxiety, and interviewer credibility: An example of cognitive balance in a dyad. *Journal of Counseling Psychology, 19* (5), 173-177.

Williamson, E. G. (1966). Value options and the counseling relationship. *The Personnel and Guidance Journal, 44,* 617-623.

Wolberg, L. R. (1954). *The Technique of Psychotherapy.* New York: Greene and Stratton.

# Part IV

# PRACTICAL TECHNIQUES

PART **IV**

# PRACTICAL TECHNIQUES

The practical techniques which are explained in this Part IV will be employed more effectively if the counselor has an understanding of the frame of reference with which many alcoholics operate. By frame of reference the author refers to where the alcoholic is coming from emotionally, spiritually, and intellectually.

## A FRAME OF REFERENCE

As was noted in Part III only those individuals who have resolved genuinely to stop drinking can profit from counseling. More often than not this resolution is a function of having lived and identified with the Twelve Steps of Alcoholics Anonymous. More often than not these Steps are the alcoholic's frame of reference and not uncommonly, provide initial topics for explanation and discussion in counseling.

The prospective counselor who is a recovering alcoholic knows the Steps, has reflected, meditated on them, and lived with them.

The counselor who is not a recovering alcoholic may not be familiar with the Steps. It is the author's conviction that the effective counselor, recovering alcoholic or not, is one who knows what these Steps are and is concerned with what they mean to the client. Quite generally, the counselor who has an intellectual and emotional appreciation of the Twelve Steps finds that rapport with the client invariably comes early. More importantly, once the counselor has learned how the client interprets the steps he/she has obtained an invaluable window into the client's system of thought and emotional life too.

The interpretations which follow the first five Steps are the author's. Hopefully, counselors who are familiar with the Steps and have developed their own interpretations for these, will find more food for reflection. Counselors who are not familiar with the Steps are encouraged to explore other interpretations and finally develop their own subjective meaning.

**Step One**

*"We admitted we were powerless over alcohol, that our lives had become unmanageable."*

Taking this first step is critical if one is to change and redevelop his/her personality. The view here is that a healthy nonalcoholic personality can be built only upon a foundation of avowed human weakness. The person who is not able to admit to a lack of control toward drink cannot expect to recover in any substantial way. A person who is unable to attain a meaningful sobriety is precisely one who has not been able to admit to innate powerlessness.

Acceptance of this first step is excruciatingly difficult because it is an admission that one has lost control over one's own self. Many cannot accept this first step because by doing so they feel that they become "losers" in their own eyes.

This first Step can best be understood as an avowed, external admission of long time internal feelings of weakness and ineffectuality. The denial and rationalization defenses have kept these internal feelings from surfacing. In most cases an acute sense of desperation is what tears them down. The process of restructuring and altering these defenses is an important focal point of the early counseling session.

**Step Two**

*"Came to believe that a Power greater than ourselves could restore us to sanity."*

This Step is conducive to restructuring of defenses. Why? Because with acceptance of this Step the alcoholic begins to perceive a whole new world and comes to understand that physical and emotional energy need not be directed inwardly, need not be focused upon personal inadequacies and failures but rather, can be directed externally. Via this Step the alcoholic comes to understand that investment in one's fellow human, God, in whatever context, or the cosmos generally can reap rich and enhancing dividends. Implied in this Step is that every individual must have an object upon which to attach faith. Without such an attachment self-esteem and a continuing self-enhancement are not possible.

Implied too, in this Step is that the alcoholic who comes to accept this step admits to an emotional life in shambles and a distorted system of thought. Simply, the alcoholic admits to a life which has been lived insanely. Heretofore energies have been channeled into maintaining that insanity. With acceptance of this second Step the alcoholic is in a position to return to a sane life.

**Step Three**

*"Make a decision to turn our will and our lives over to the care of God as we understand him."*

Steps One and Two lead the alcoholic away from an exaggerated concern with one's self and encourage physical and emotional energies externally. Both steps are meditative, reflective, and oblige only acceptance. Step Three obliges the alcoholic to act on the acceptance of the first two Steps.

The key to acceptance of Step Three is motivation. The alcoholic who is motivated toward investment in God will be successful. The definition and interpretation of God is left to the particular individual. For many this definition is the fellowship of Alcoholics Anonymous. To this fellowship many submit their will and their lives.

Via this Step then, the individual comes to be dependent upon A.A. Such a dependence he/she comes to believe results in an independence of spirit and a more emotionally relaxed life. What this author has learned is that clients who have accepted this third Step develop a more optimistic perception of problem situations. More importantly, people are viewed more tolerantly and interaction with the alcoholic invariably becomes more rewarding.

**Step Four**

*"Made a searching and fearless moral inventory of ourselves."*

The desire to fully achieve this Step leads many alcoholics into counseling. The traditional A.A. interpretation of this Step is based upon an understanding and control of the basic human instincts. In the A.A. view instincts unbridled are conducive to self-destruction.

The author has utilized the client's interest in this Step differently. Thus, the counselor has encouraged the client to focus on those aspects of his/her personality which are of special concern. This counselor has found that general and basic psychological needs—security, love, self-esteem, and self-actualization—have provided an effective framework in which to help the client better understand his/her specific concerns and anxieties and those instincts from which they spring. What the author has found too, is that the alcoholic penchants for excess, guilt, and mood swings stem from a lack of understanding of the basic human search for satisfaction of these needs. This Step Four seems to be best achieved by clients when they come to have a clear understanding of what self-esteem means to them.

**Step Five**

*"Admitted to God, to ourselves and to another human being the exact nature of our wrongs."*

The A.A. view here is that "confession is good for the soul." Such a view not only promotes the counseling enterprise but may even facilitate rapport. The author's experience has been that clients who are strongly identified with this fifth Step are positively anxious to "spill their guts." These clients seem especially eager to explain in graphic detail those incidents where they inflicted pain upon others.

For such clients the counseling session is perceived as an opportunity for an emotional catharsis. And it is. Clients at the end of a draining session almost always feel better. (A positive by-product is that rapport and the client-counselor relationship are almost always strengthened.) But the counselor should be very much aware that catharsis while beneficial is not in itself the end-all of the counseling process. Catharses are at best temporary. Their value lies in *precipitating* insight and in turn, change. Very often clients in general, alcoholics in particular, have shared their most intimate experiences and conflicts and even convincingly explained to this counselor the why of their drinking—and then proceeded to engage in the same destructive behavior! In short catharsis, *even catharsis complemented with insight, is no guarantee of positive change especially in the alcoholic client. Only when the client genuinely finds reward in change will he/she be and stay on the road to recovery.*

**Note:** Steps Six through Twelve are reproduced verbatim for the benefit of those counselors who are not familiar with them. They were not interpreted because the author felt that their content was not conducive to any meaningful interpretation for the counselor-client process. The A.A. interpretations can be obtained from the manual *Twelve Steps and Twelve Traditions,* Alcoholics Anonymous World Services Inc., 468 Park Avenue South, New York, N.Y. 10016.

**Step Six**

*"We're entirely ready to have God remove all these defects of character."*

**Step Seven**

*"Humbly asked Him to remove our shortcomings."*

**Step Eight**

*"Made a list of all persons we had harmed, and became willing to make amends to them all."*

**Step Nine**

*"Made direct amends to such people wherever possible, except when to do so would injure them or others."*

**Step Ten**

*"Continued to take personal inventory and when we were wrong promptly admitted to it."*

**Step Eleven**

*"Sought through prayer and meditation to improve our conscious contact with God, as we understood Him, praying only for knowledge of His will for us and the power to carry that out."*

**Step Twelve**

*"Having had a spiritual awakening as the result of these steps, we tried to carry this message to alcoholics, and to practice these principles in all our affairs."*

## REDIRECTING AND RESTRUCTURING DEFENSES

As noted in Part I, helping the alcoholic client to restructure his/her system of defense is a critical task of the counselor. In many of the illustrations which follow, notably confrontation, the reader will be able to see that this process typically is woven together with other client issues. Examples which follow are simulated in order to focus specifically on the issue of defense. The counselor style depicted melds directivist with nondirectivist.

**Denial and Rationalization**

These two defenses are treated together because they often occur in tandem with rationalization serving as a support for denial. A common phenomenon among newly recovering alcoholics is the refusal to acknowledge their real competencies. Such is the case here.

CL *I think I've decided not to take the office supervisor job.*

CO *Oh?*

CL *I honestly don't think I'm ready for it.*

CO *I'm confused.*

CL *Why?*

CO *Yesterday you said you were going to take it. You told me you were looking forward to going back to it.*

CL *I changed my mind.*

CO *What changed it?*

CL *I'm just not ready for it.*

CO *I was under the impression you were a supervisor for almost twenty years.*

CL *I was and look what happened! I became a drunk.*

CO *You became a drunk because you were the office supervisor?* (A hint of incredulity in the tone would not be inappropriate.)

CL *Well, it contributed to it. People, women especially, are a bitch to work with. If I were a man I wouldn't hesitate—women respect men more.*

CO (Grinning) *It's because you're not a man that you can't be a supervisor at this time. You don't feel you command enough respect.*

CL *You think I'm making excuses, don't you?*

CO *Aren't you? Janice, the reality is that you functioned for twenty years as a supervisor and the last five you were drunk a good part of the time.*

CL *And if I did it drunk I can do it sober, eh?*

CO *What do you think?*

What the counselor does here is to focus on the client's denial, repeating, rephrasing and always focusing on what the client is saying to help her see that her vacillation is founded upon the just plain fear that she can't do what she's already done for a couple of decades.

**Displacement**

Occasionally, clients will ventilate anger. More often than not, this counselor's response has been simply an acceptance of the client and his/her feelings. To respond with anger is grossly inappropriate. The view is that the follow-up session to the ventilation, sometimes during the same session if clients are feeling remorseful, is the more critical point in the therapy. What the counselor has to communicate to clients is that while anger is a legitimate emotion, when displayed it doesn't serve to enhance personality. What the counselor has to communicate, too, is that what angry clients usually feel is a function of other disquieting and troubling circumstances of their lives. More importantly, that they have to deal with those people and situations which have engendered that anger.

**Fantasy**

What clients daydream about, what they wish for is important. Fantasizing can be more than a simple escape from boredom or harsh reality. It can be a springboard to creativity. Certainly fantasy does not have to be destructive as it may have been for alcoholics during their drinking days.

Alcoholics, particularly those who seek to share their fantasies, need to hear these ideas. And when they begin talking about some of their wishes and dreams, the sensitive counselor will do more than listen. He/she should help clients to evaluate the feasibility of translating fantasies into reality.

**Projection**

The suspicious client is not easy to deal with and many alcoholics are very suspicious. Too often it is a major aspect of alcoholic makeup. The best counselor antidote for suspiciousness in alcoholic clients is reliability and trustworthiness. A promise, or appointment should never be made with the client unless the counselor knows full well that he/she can keep it. Authenticity and candor also are excellent antidotes. Nothing feeds and expands this defense as much as game playing.

Clients who project are exquisitely sensitive to verbal nuances, body movements, a simple sigh. If a usually engaging client asks the counselor if the latter is anxious to terminate an interview when he/she is, the counselor can answer honestly *"I am but it's got nothing to do with you. I found out a half hour ago that I'm the one who has to pick up my son at the sitter's because my spouse got hung up in town."* An honest explanation punctuated with a chuckle and even a compliment, *"I thought I was hiding my nervousness. You're very perceptive"* will help the client to see that his/her perception is accurate and to express it under such circumstances is perfectly O.K.

**Regression**

Regression as was noted in Part I is characterized by immature behavior and is often manipulative. The counselor's task is to communicate that the behavior effected by his/her defense is seldom attractive and more often than not will alienate other people. The illustration which follows exemplifies a situation which has occurred a number of times with the author.

CO *I'm sorry, John, I can't do it. I'm not going to serve as your job agent. You'll have to make the call yourself.*

CL *What's the big deal?*

CO *It's a big deal. You'll have to set up the interview yourself.*

CL (Yells) *I thought you were here to help me.*

CO (Quietly) *I am. I'm here to help you help yourself.*

CL (Sulking) *What a crock this place is. All they tell you here is that they want to help. You ask for help and you get a lot of horseshit explanations.*

CO *Not horseshit. It's true. We're, I'm here to help you help yourself.*

CL (Cries out) *So! Help me!*

CO (Quietly) *John, a man who whines like a baby does not endear himself to people.*

CL (Grimly) *Man, you can take this place, your psychology too, and roll it up into a big fat ball and shove it, man, shove it.*

(Slams out)

Next day

CL (Sheepishly) *I made the call. I got an interview at two o'clock today.*

CO *Good!*

CL *I'm scared, man, I'm scared.*

CO *Aren't we all: Let's talk.*

**Repression**

Repression is the defense which clients may well have employed immoderately in their past. Too often the effect has been to leave them scared, immature and unsure of themselves. Rather than attempt to deal with whys and whens of the repression, this counselor has found it more productive to help the client build other defenses. Two which seem to address themselves to the debilitating effects of repression are compensation and sublimation. In the former, clients are encouraged to look for and identify with situations, hobbies, events where they can find some reward and demonstrate some measure of success to their own selves. Similarly, sublimation involves directing energy in the service of others and one's own healthy self. Alcoholism programs especially provide ample opportunity for the development of both defenses.

## SILENCE

Silence is often threatening to counselors, even thoroughly competent ones. They became anxious, seeing a protracted pause as a symptom of their ineptitude. Not understanding the many excellent reasons for it, they break it clumsily and thereby communicate their anxiety and in turn increase the client's discomfort.

**Why Silences Occur**

1. **Embarrassment** is a major reason silences occur especially at the initial contact. Clients do not know what to say. The initial contact with the alcoholism counselor may well be their first experience with counseling. The most alcoholics know, and this in a dim way, is that they are supposed to confide and share innermost feelings, fears, and fantasies, something clients might be willing to do but do not know how and simply, they are too embarrassed to begin.

2. **Resentment, hostility, and anger** are all reasons why silences occur. This is especially true in the mandated referral. The counselor is perceived as an agent of the person making the referral. What the alcoholic sees is that he/she is being victimized by the court, the parole officer, or whoever. The client then releases his/her hostility in a passive way—by keeping mum.

3. **Testing of the counselor** is another reason for the silence. The alcoholic, it will be remembered, often has a disposition toward paranoia. The silence may well be a response to that. By keeping silent, letting the counselor do the talking, the client can size up the counselor better. In addition, the client can evauate the counselor's reaction. This client knows full well that he/she has some kind of responsibility to talk and share. And the client knows that the silence can precipitate a variety of reactions in the counselor: impatience, anger, embarrassment, etc. And so he/she tests. This interpersonal stance by the alcoholic may well be habitual and not even conscious.

4. **Conflict** is another reason for the silence. More often than not, alcoholics are emotionally betwixt and between. They don't know what to say, where to start, precisely because there is so very much to say. And so clients sit tongue-tied, helpless, victims of their own emotional conflicts. Such clients often perspire, fidget, twitch.

5. **Fear** is a major reason for silence, especially at the initial contact. The counselor finally is just another stranger, and typically, alcoholics have learned that most people are simply not that caring. Moreover, at some level all clients understand that a purpose of the counseling is to

change them, and note, no human beings ever delight in that idea. On the contrary most people are scared by any potential change in themselves. They know what they have. Who knows what change will bring? This kind of feeling is a major reason alcoholics persevere in their drinking.

6. **Integration** by the client of what he/she or the counselor has said. Counseling can be painfully emotional, even traumatic at times, and some clients need time to absorb it all. A silence for some clients is simply a manifestation of that need.

7. **The end of a topic** may produce silence. Sometimes a silence occurs because counselor and client have finished a long discussion. There is a pause while the client searches for a relevant topic.

### Handling the Silence

Once the counselor understands that the silence is a product of complex client dynamics it should be less threatening. In any case, he/she should be better equipped to deal with it. Some of the specific reasons for a silence (at times there are several reasons) are easy to discern, others are more difficult. The counselor's ability to fathom and deal with these more indiscernible reasons will test both his/her clinical skills and perceptual sensitivity. Following are some suggestions for dealing with differently motivated silences.

1. **Embarrassment** is easy to detect. Confrontation usually aggravates it. The better approach is a comment or question manifestly unrelated to the client's alcoholism but about the client and/or his/her interests (A look into his/her background before the first session is always helpful). The question might focus on a hobby, his/her work, family, and so forth.

2. **Resentment, hostility, or anger** is very apparent. A gentle-like confrontation is appropriate. In the case of the mandated referral, a comment like this might be helpful: *"John, I know you were sent here and quite apparently you're not happy. Just know that I'm here to help, if you want it. And I know real well I can't make you open up if you don't want to. Whenever you're ready."* When a mandated referral is not the reason, confrontation is still appropriate. "John, you're not happy. I'm sorry for that. Just know that I'm here to help if you want it . . ." and so forth.

3. **Testing** of the counselor can occur for various reasons. This motive for silence is not always easy to detect and when the counselor genuinely is puzzled as to the why of the silence, probing with neutral comments is in order, i.e., *"Sometimes it's tough to talk,"* or *"You're quiet today. Do you know why?"* Under no circumstances should the counselor launch into chit-chat. If the counselor concludes because of the client's facial expressions, body language, and just feelings that the client's silence is a function of hostility, then the counselor should lean back, smile appropriately, shrug, and say to the client, *"Whenever you're ready is okay with me."* The idea is to communicate patience and receptivity.

4. **Conflict** is very apparent. Reassuring comments delivered softly with warmth are usually beneficial and ultimately move the client to talk.

5. **Fear** once detected and it's not difficult to do so, is dealt with in pretty much the same fashion as one would deal with conflict.

6. **Integration** by the client of ideas, concepts, insights, and personality components often produce silence. This silence is best left alone as the client is in the process of absorbing what he/she is feeling or has just learned. A comment by the counselor serves no purpose, a question would be even worse.

7. **The end of a thought** expressed by the client may cause silence. The author has let this silence go on with the new client hoping he/she would break it and thereby assume more of the responsibility for the counseling. He has not let it go on if the client was becoming embarrassed. Nor has he let it go on when the rapport and progress are solid. Under these latter circumstances this counselor breaks silence with a comment like, *"Well, what thoughts are you having?"* If the client responds with none, the counselor will break the silence by referring back to something the client said previously.

## LEARNING ACTIVITIES

The following activities on learning to deal effectively with silence and those which come immediately after each of the subsequent techniques illustrate activities which the prospective and inservice counselor can utilize to both learn and upgrade counselor skills. These activities are in outline form and can be modified, expanded, or revised to meet local training needs. Any alterations however, should retain the requisite elements of any effective learning exercise. These are

Justification,
Purpose,
Objectives/Outcomes,
Specific Activities, and
Evaluation Methods.

## STUDENT ACTIVITIES FOR LEARNING TO DEAL EFFECTIVELY WITH SILENCE

### Justification

Protracted pauses may generate anxiety in the counselor and/or the client. Learning to deal with the silence can abate that anxiety and facilitate counseling.

### Purposes

1. To expand the student counselor's theoretical knowledge about the element of silence in counseling.

2. To develop and sharpen the student counselor's practical skill to deal effectively with silence.

### Outcome

Student counselor demonstrates that he/she can indeed handle silence.

### Specific Activities

1. Verification that the student counselor knows theoretical reasons why silences occur in counseling.

2. Verification that the student counselor knows possible and varied ways to handle silence.

3. Student counselor views video demonstrations on how to handle silence.

4. Student counselor views live demonstrations by mentor on how to handle silence.

5. Student counselor engages in role playing with the mentor.

6. Student counselor views videotaping of himself/herself counseling session with new client.

### Evaluation

1. Feedback from mentor and student colleagues.

2. Activities continue until student counselor and mentor are mutually satisfied with student counselor's performance.

## LISTENING

### Prefatory Comments

Moustakas (1966) has observed that "When we are listened to, it creates us, makes us unfold and expand." Most alcoholic clients have never learned how to unfold and expand precisely because they feel that no one ever really listened to them. This feeling has contributed much toward their suspiciousness, their anger, and their penchant for testing others. The counselor who listens, in a word, enhances. Such a counselor provides the alcoholic with a rare opportunity to unfold and expand.

Patterson (1959) believed that listening is "the basic, most universal, most important technique in counseling and psychotherapy." If listening isn't the most important technique, it is certainly critical. Without this ability the counselor will find meaningful rapport is impossible.

Effective listening is sometimes difficult even for competent, experienced counselors. In the emotionally charged climate of counseling it is easy to ask inappropriate questions, to offer unasked for, unneeded advice, to interrupt with an irrelevant interpretation, or to supply a well intended but unnecessary supportive remark. Behaviors like these communicate a lack of interest, tell the client that the counselor is not listening; and the counselor who doesn't listen is one who is meeting his/her own needs, not those of the client.

**Aspects of Listening**

The listening counselor not only hears the client's words but also is exquisitely sensitive to his/her feelings, tones, and sounds made. Feelings and tones carry the real meaning of words and reflect the emotions of the client. Such tones Westcott (1966) has termed *phasis.* The counselor who is finely attuned to the *phasis* in client talk is the one who can get close. Thus in his/her responses the counselor can, should address the emotion the client is feeling as well as the verbal content expressed, i.e., *"I believe you, Bill. That crackle in your voice tells me real well how angry you really are."*

The counselor also should be fully aware of sounds which a client makes, like finger drumming, hand clapping, even making chair squeak with his/her constant shifting. Westcott (1966) has termed such sounds *strepitus.* They speak much about the client's internal anxiety. To respond to them or not would be dependent upon the quality of rapport existing between counselor and alcoholic. If the rapport is good, a comment whimsically made might be very appropriate, i.e., *"That's a regular tatoo you're doing there. It's even got a regular beat."* In sum, a response to feeling tones, to sounds made by the client demonstrate in a concrete way how well attuned the counselor is to the client's presence and to everything about him/her.

**Listening Techniques**

For the counselor to listen is not enough, he/she also needs to communicate his/her motivation to do so. Following are some practical suggestions to accomplish this communication.

1. How the counselor *sits* communicates much about motivation to listen. And how the counselor sits is really a function of personality.

Some counselors are more formal or casual than others. Simply, one should sit so he/she is comfortable. Counselor comfort will communicate and set a comfortable tone for the encounter. The counselor should sit, of course, so the client can be observed directly. This author who leans back and puts his feet atop the desk, has never been able to appreciate Freud's method to sit behind the head of the lying down client.

2. The counselor should structure the counseling hour so *no interruptions* occur. A phone for incoming calls should be programmed for transfer to another phone. If this isn't possible, it might be feasible to have the phone put on a jack so it can be pulled out for the counseling hour. Hanging out a "Do Not Disturb" sign is eminently appropriate. All these procedures will serve to communicate to the client this important idea—you are the focus of my attention.

3. In order to listen at his/her best the counselor should develop the ability to *isolate distracting* thoughts. This idea was explained fully in Part III under "Obstacles to Establishment of Rapport." A rereading of that section might be helpful.

4. The counselor will not be able to listen attentively if he/she is not fully cognizant of *topics and words* which precipitate a negative reaction internally. Certain words and subjects are emotionally laden for some people and counselors are no exception. This fact was illustrated in dramatic fashion to this author about a year ago. The alcoholic at the very first session told this counselor an ethnic joke, followed with another about blacks. The counselor overlooked them figuring they were a function of the client's anxiety, perhaps some kind of testing, and so forth. At the next session the client opened with a particularly tasteless story about blacks. This counselor let down his guard and winced. The client became embarrassed and asked if he had been offensive. When told he had, the client became angry and left. He returned later that day and apologized, finished with the rationalization, *"We're all different!"* However, he never made another racial slur.

In this instance it all worked out okay. However, had the author better known what his feelings were he would not have winced, would not have had to say he was offended, and thereby come near to losing the client. However strong one's feelings might be regarding the obscenity and foolishness too, of prejudice, the counseling session is simply not a forum for instruction in healthier race relations.

5. The counselor who asks focused, pertinent *questions* will demonstrate that he/she is listening. The questions should always be derived from the client's comments and should never introduce a new topic. Questions unrelated to what the client is discussing ordinarily reflect inattention, boredom, and general uninterest. This whole topic of questioning is developed more fully in the next section.

## ACTIVITIES FOR LEARNING LISTENING SKILLS

### Justification

Counseling is not possible if the counselor does not know how to listen. Effective counseling is enhanced mightily by a counselor who is a skilled listener.

### Purposes

1. To increase the student counselor's theoretical knowledge about listening in counseling.

2. To develop and increase the student counselor's practical listening skills.

### Outcome

The student counselor demonstrates that he/she has acquired listening skills.

### Specific Activities

1. Verification that the student counselor knows reasons why counselor listening can be blocked.

2. Verification that the student counselor knows how effective listening can be enhanced.

3. View video demonstration of counselors who are effective listeners.

4. View live demonstrations by mentor counselor.

5. Role play with mentor counselor or colleagues.

6. Student counselor views himself/herself on video tape.

**Evaluation**

1. Student counselor obtains feedback from mentor, colleagues, and clients.

2. Activities continue until mentor and student are mutually satisfied that student counselor is an effective listener.

## QUESTIONING

**Problems**

Questions, especially with alcoholics, may have certain problems. By the questions very nature they are designed to elicit information, information which the client can consider too private to share. They may touch on areas which engender fear. In short, a basic problem with questions is that they probe into the unknown.

Questions for some counselors too often lead to more questions. Too often the counseling takes on the spectacle of a courtroom with the counselor playing the role of a prosecuting attorney. A barrage of questions can turn counselor and client into adversaries.

Questions have another potential disadvantage. Clients may become conditioned to think in terms of answering questions, not in terms of sharing, expressing voluntarily, self-examining. In short, their sense of responsibility for counseling may become stultified.

Finally questioning *per se* has another major disadvantage; too often it focuses upon the cognitive domain rather than upon feelings. Cognitive understanding is helpful even desirable but without emotional appreciation the cognitive understanding has little value for the client. Under such circumstances, meaningful insight is simply not possible.

**Positive Aspects**

Despite these limitations, thoughtful questioning can be helpful and facilitative. It can serve as a lead into productive discussion. Clear, succinct, gently toned questions ordinarily are not inappropriate if the counselor derives them from the client's comments and discussion.

Questions posed should always be open-ended. After posing the question, the counselor should wait for the client's response. Therein will lie the validity and fruitfulness of the counselor's query.

Following are two illustrations. In this scene the client has been talking nonstop for almost ten minutes.

**Inappropriate Use of Questions**

CL . . . *anyways like I was saying I know I have to take each day at a time and I'm doing that but I think I can start making plans to get out of here. I've been sober for two months now and I want to thank you. You've really helped me.*

CO *Why are you banging on the table like that?*

CL (Laughs) *I'm nervous.*

CO *Why are you nervous?*

CL (Shrugs) *I don't know, the way you're looking at me makes me nervous, makes me feel like a gold fish in a bowl . . . . .* (Client's talk continues aimlessly for several minutes.)

CO *Why are you talking so much today? And why are you banging on the table again?*

CL *Like I said, I'm nervous.*

CO *You're getting ready to blow it, aren't you?*

CL *You know damn well I'm not.*

CO *Then how come I didn't see you yesterday?*

CL *I told you about that.*

This counselor broke the rules of good questioning. His/her questions were not founded on client comment. He/she asked a second question before he/she got an answer to the first. He/she sounded a little bit like an anxious but determined prosecuting attorney, even his/her observation of client table drumming sounded more like accusations than gently toned comments designed to communicate an accepting confirmation of the client's hyperactive behavior.

**Appropriate Use of Questions**

The following scene opens exactly as the first did.

CL *. . . Anyways like I was saying I know I have to take each day at a time and I'm doing that but I think I can start making plans to get out of here. I've been sober for two months now. And I want to thank you. You've really helped me.*

CO *That's why I'm here. To help. How exactly have I helped?*

CL (Drumming hand on the desk) *Well you're not like some of the other guys around here, always on your back, buzzing around, asking questions, trying to get into your head. Al's got a counselor like that, always asking him if he's building up to drink.*

CO (Smiles) *Should I ask you that?*

CL *Sure ask.*

CO (Seriously) *Are you building up to a drink?*

CL *No!* (Slams the desk)

CO *Would you say this beating you're giving the desk today is the you that you were a week ago?*

CL (Silent for a moment. Sighs) *You know, huh?*

CO (Nods) *I know.*

CL *I'm dying, doc.*

CO (Smiling) *Let's talk about it.*

Both counselors were very aware that the client's behavior was symptomatic of BUD. The second one's use of questions aimed at letting the client know of his awareness without making him defensive and getting him to talk. In sum, a counselor's questions should not be merely a reaction to a client's specific comment. They should have an ultimate purpose too. In this instance it was to get the client to discuss his craving.

## ACTIVITIES FOR LEARNING QUESTIONING SKILLS

**Justification**

The counselor who questions effectively demonstrates interest in the client, reinforces rapport, and generally facilitates the counseling progress.

**Purposes**

1. To increase the student counselor's theoretical knowledge about the technique of questions.

2. To develop and sharpen the student counselor's questioning skills.

**Outcome**

Student counselor demonstrates that he/she has the ability to question effectively.

**Specific Activities**

1. Verification that the student counselor is familiar with the theory of positive and negative aspects of questioning.

2. Verification that the student counselor knows appropriate and inappropriate use of questioning.

3. View examples of effective counselor questioning on video tape.

4. View live demonstrations of effective questioning.

5. Role play with mentor or colleagues.

6. Student counselor views video tape of himself/herself questioning in a counseling session.

**Evaluation**

1. Student counselor obtains feedback from mentor, colleagues, and client.

2. Demonstrations continue until counselor and client are mutually agreed that student is an effective questioner.

## REITERATION OF CONTENT

**Definition**

Reiteration refers to a literal restatement or a rephrasing by the counselor of what the client said. When the counselor does this restatement, he/she is telling the client that he/she understands. Ordinarily when the counselor reiterates no attempt is made to interpret the meaning of what the client said.

**Explanation**

Reiteration as a technique serves many useful purposes. It immediately puts the counselor into an accepting role, thereby facilitating both rapport and communication. It invariably elicits client feelings conducive to better cognitive understanding. Reiteration helps clients to focus and delineate their thinking. It can help clients reconsider both thinking and viewpoint, i.e., when the counselor reiterates with an inquisitive or honestly puzzled look. Another prime value of reiteration is then, to help clients to crystallize their thoughts.

The following two examples illustrate this technique. The client is an alcoholic wife and mother in her early thirties. This excerpt was taken from a tape and was edited by the author.

**Directivist—Illustrative Excerpt**

CL *You can't help me, not in this.*

CO *When you open like that I know you want to talk. So talk and try me.*

(Pause)

CL *He's having an affair.* (She starts crying.)

CO *Your husband's screwing around on you.*

CL *Yes. Bastard. When I really needed his support. Instead of help I get degraded.*

CO *The bastard degraded you.*

CL *God, it's enough to make me want to blow it.*

CO *You want to get blind, stinking drunk.*

CL (Screams) *I won't! I won't!*

CO *You won't if you don't want to.*

CL *I want to. He said his life was hell when I was drinking. God knows I want to make his life hell again for what he's done to me.*

CO *You want to make his life hell for degrading you. Drinking will punish the bastard.*

CL *And it will too!*

**Nondirectivist—Illustrative Excerpt**

The following illustration is a simulation of the preceding excerpt.

CL *You can't help me not in this.*

CO *You don't feel I can help you. You may be right.*

CO *I'm here to try if you want me to.*

(Pause)

CL *He's having an affair.* (Cries)

CO *John is having an affair.*

CL *Yes. Bastard. When I really needed his support. Instead of help I get degraded.*

CO *Right in this time that you need support the most, he degrades you.*

CL *God, it's enough to make me want to blow it.*

CO *It's enough to make you want to return to drink.*

CL *I want to. He said his life was hell when I was drinking. God knows I want to make his life hell.*

CO *You want his life to be hell for what he's done to you.*

### Comments on Illustrative Excerpts

Both counselors did a creditable job. The nondirectivist as usual is a little less blunt, a little less emotional, and a little more literal in his reiteration. The directivist tends more toward colorful rephrasing, is more inclined toward the supportive remark, *"You won't if you don't want to."* Both did well to focus and respond to the client's statement and neither did any interpreting.

## ACTIVITIES FOR LEARNING HOW TO REITERATE CONTENT

### Justification

The counselor who can reiterate well is one who facilitates both rapport and communication.

### Purposes

1. To heighten the student counselor's awareness of the effectiveness and benefits of the reiteration technique.

2. To sharpen the student counselor's ability to reiterate content.

### Outcome

Student counselor is effective in ability to reiterate content in an actual counseling session.

### Specific Activities

1. Verification that student counselor knows theory underlying when and how to reiterate content.

2. View excerpts of model counselor reiterating on video tapes.

3. View live demonstrations of reiterating.

4. Role playing with colleagues, with mentor, observing.

5. Student counselor observes self reiterating on video.

6. Student counselor demonstrates ability to reiterate in live counseling sessions.

### Evaluation

1. Student counselor obtains feedback from mentor, colleagues, and so forth.

2. Student counselor continues activities until counselor and mentor are both satisfied with performance.

## REFLECTION OF FEELING

### Definition and Value

Reflection of feeling is closely allied to the concept of empathy. When counselors reflect feeling they communicate that they understand and perceive what clients are experiencing and feeling.

Reflection of feeling is among the least threatening of counselor techniques because the focus is on emotions and not intellectual content. It involves no questioning, no verbal pushing, the counselor merely mirrors tones and feelings expressed by the client. Highlen and Baccus (1977) in a study with forty women found this technique was very effective in both eliciting and clarifying self-referenced emotion.

Counselors who reflect feelings effectively invariably lead the client into self-confrontation. And clients who hear and feel feelings come back at them are made to realize that their feelings are important, legitimate, and not crazy at all. Why? Another human being has understood and mirrored them.

The major benefit of this technique is not only in clients crystallizing their feelings but in understanding their feelings *in relation to people.* Feelings which trouble the most, of course, are those which have to do with relationships.

Alcoholics who come for counseling are usually very confused about relationships. They are laden with anger, guilt, and/or fear about them. As their feelings become clarified, self-understanding in relation to others becomes more ordered, more logical, more healthful. The change though gradual is usually discernible as it is reflected in clients' talk, general manner, even appearance.

**Language**

The counselor should try to use the language easily understood by the client. This counselor's preference is to use the same words as the client, varying only to avoid sounding like "Little Sir Echo." In any case, pretentious terminology always should be avoided.

**Client Enhancement**

Clarification of feeling enhances the client in two important ways. When feelings are reflected to them clients come to see that feelings more often than not are *causes* of much dysfunctional behavior. In coming to see this, frequently clients ultimately see something more important—that they can cause their behavior, that they do not have to be victims, and, if they are, the reason is because they choose to be. The development of this way of thinking is vital if the alcoholic is to begin to recover.

The counselor can be most effective when reflecting feelings if certain points are kept in mind.

**Feelings Hide Feelings**

The counselor should address only the feelings presented by the client. At the same time it should be born in mind that the obvious feelings are not always the most important ones. Many clients mask their more debilitating feelings with other ones. The author recalls a female alcoholic, for example, who punctuated every third sentence with a sharp, nervous laugh to mask her anger and guilt.

## Timing

Too often counselors wait for a client to finish a rather lengthy verbalization and miss much important affect. Feelings should be reflected as soon as possible after they are expressed.

Once the client has come to see that feelings cause behavior, he/she invariably begins an examination of precipitating *motives.* Such an examination can only lead to a better self-appreciation.

Clarification of feeling is essentially a technique of the Rogerian nondirectivist school. The illustration which follows is by a follower of that school. The edited excerpt is drawn from four sessions. These tapes are from a colleague's library.

## Illustration of Reflection of Feelings

CL *I'm going to have to stop drinking. I know it.*

CO *Your tone says that you don't want to.*

CL *I do. It's just that my husband and my daughter . . . but they're right, I know they are.*

CO *They're pressuring you, making you feel guilty.*

CL *Yes, especially my daughter. My daughter had such a look of horror in her face when she caught me pouring a drink.*

CO *And so the guilt. You wanted to die.*

CL *Yes, I did. And I made it worse. I screamed at her for tip-toeing. I've got a tip-toer for a daughter. She never wears shoes in the house only those damn slipper socks. It's like she haunts the house, always materializing out of nowhere.*

CO *She tip-toes around, materializes out of nowhere, and makes you feel guilty and angry 'cause you can't have a drink whenever you want.*

CL *My husband's worse. He just lectures me. I have to account for every damn penny now. It's hard saving money for booze out of the grocery money. And he lectures me right in front of her. How do you think that makes me feel?*

CO *Humiliated and then angry too, I'll bet.*

CL *Yes, and the humiliation is hurting my daughter, too. I've told him that. I've told him I've got to want to stop myself and he's only making it worse with his damned sermons.*

CO *He makes you so mad that you want to keep drinking.*

CL *Yes. Honestly, sometimes when I'm alone and drinking I feel like I hate the two of them for what they're doing to me.*

CO *Drink makes you feel you hate them.*

CL *I'm not so sure it's the drink that does it. Sometimes even when I'm sober I hate them. Like right now.*

CO *Right now you feel you hate them.*

CL *I think like that a lot. Really it's why I started. I'm convinced of that. You know that old line about being driven to drink? It's not so crazy, not so crazy. They drive me to drink, the two of them, him with his sermons and her watching me like a hawk.*

CO *I can appreciate how being watched like a hawk would make you angry. It would me.*

CL (Crying) *God I was so awful. I made a real ass of myself.* (Pause) *We went to our annual family reunion and I got drunk. The whole thing's a blur for me. I don't remember too much only that I tried to dance on a picnic table while people ate and I fell off. I remember looking up and the looks, the awful looks, and a woman's voice saying, "She's a drunken bum." The last thing I remember is driving home in the car and my daughter was sobbing. Right then I wanted to die. I had humiliated my husband, my daughter, and me. Drunk, drunk as I was, I cried. Believe it or not for the first time in my life I got a good look at myself in the awful looks, in that woman's sneer, "She's a drunken bum," and in my daughter's tears. You have to know she never cries. I made her cry.*

CO *Her tears made you see yourself better.*

CL (High pitched voice) *It's not them I hate, it's me. I hate me and what I'm doing to them and to me. I hate myself. I hate myself for how I look, too puffy in the face, too big in the stomach—all vodka and gin. It's me I hate, not them.*

### Comments on Illustrative Excerpt

It's very difficult to fully appreciate this or any effective counselor via the printed word. On the tape the counselor's tones gibed perfectly with those of the client. The reader can still learn from this excerpt though. The counselor didn't use the stereotypic lines *"What you're feeling is"* or *"You feel . . ."* Instead the counselor focused on the client's feelings and her words by reusing them, paraphrasing them, and by reinforcing the validity of her dramatic self-confrontation. It is fair to assume that the counselor's knowledge and exquisite sensitivity probably convinced him at the outset that her avowed hate of both husband and daughter were only a mask for her own self-hate and a prop for her denial of the love she really felt for them.

## ACTIVITIES FOR LEARNING HOW TO REFLECT FEELING

### Justification

The ability to reflect feeling effectively is a critically important skill in counseling because it is via this technique that the counselor is able to communicate empathy.

### Purposes

1. To heighten and reinforce the student counselor's awareness of the importance of emotional communication in counseling.

2. To sharpen the student counselor's ability to reflect feeling.

**Outcome**

Student counselor demonstrates his/her ability to reflect feeling effectively in a real counseling session.

**Specific Activities**

1. Verification that the student counselor is thoroughly conversant with the theory behind reflection of feeling.

2. View video excerpts of professional counselors as they reflect feelings.

3. View live demonstrations of feeling reflection.

4. Role playing with colleagues and with mentor.

5. Student counselor demonstrates ability to reflect feeling in live session.

**Evaluation**

1. Feedback from mentor, colleagues.

2. Progress of his/her real clients.

3. Activities continue until mentor and student counselor are satisfied with performance.

## ROLE PLAYING

**Requirement**

The basic and only requirement in role-playing is that the participants talk, do, and try to feel as the other whose role they are playing.

### Value

The author has found role playing to be an especially valuable tool in alcoholism counseling. When this technique is utilized, alcoholics have an opportunity to become the object of their very own denials, rationalizations, and projections. This technique provides a unique learning experience for them because they see and hear in a dramatic way how they are perceived and how they relate to others and they in turn, act out the feelings they know others have toward them.

The technique should be used by counselor and client only after rapport has been established and participants feel that they know each other well. Role-playing is a novel and even exciting alternative to the regular counseling session. It is especially instructive and emotionally illuminating for the alcoholic when this technique is used with other family members. Alcoholics usually seem to be astounded to learn now much they know about a wife's, husband's, and child's feelings and interpersonal stance. More often than not, the alcoholic and his family usually seem to be emotionally rocked by the experience. The author has found no technique more effective in promoting cognitive understanding and emotional appreciation, not only of one's own problems but also of the other person's too.

## ACTIVITIES FOR LEARNING THE ART OF ROLE PLAYING

### Justification

Once the counselor has mastered this technique the alcoholism counselor can help the client to experience feelings which he/she has denied, projected, and rationalized. Via this technique too, the client experiences how he/she is perceived and can come to understand why people relate to him/her as they do.

### Purposes

1. To heighten feeling awareness in the student counselor.

2. To facilitate his/her identification with clients, (people) and thereby promote flexibility in counselor personality.

**Outcome**

Student counselor demonstrates his/her ability to role play effectively

**Specific Activities**

1. Verification that student counselor is well grounded on the theory behind the role playing technique.

2. Role playing with colleagues under mentor observation.

3. Role playing with mentor.

4. Role playing with real client with mentor observing or video-tape a role playing session with a client for self and mentor evaluation.

**Evaluation**

1. Feedback on previous four activities from mentor.

2. Activities continue until mentor and student counselor are both satisfied that skill has been attained.

## RECAPITULATION

Many alcoholics have a talent for delivering long discourses. This is true especially in the initial sessions but generally abates as the relationship strengthens and as they become healthier.

## Why the Long Discourse

The long discourses are usually a function of the usual alcoholic ailments—fear, suspicions, and unbridled anxiety. By giving a long discourse alcoholics are able to keep the counselor at a distance while they evaluate him/her. Or again, the discourse may be nothing more than a camouflage for insecurities. No matter. Whatever the reason, long monologues are not uncharacteristic of alcoholics in their initial sessions. What can the counselor do? He/she can recapitulate.

## Definition

The counselor who recapitulates responds with a focused, succinct synopsis of the client's discourse. Recapitulation then is a cognitive, intellectual activity. When counselors recapitulate they should try to use the client's words and phrases.

## Value

Recapitulation has three benefits:

- It helps to build rapport because it shows the client that the counselor is listening.

- It helps the client to focus thoughts and keep to a point or theme.

- It reinforces the counselor's own understanding.

The illustration which follows is simulated but serves to exemplify this simple but valuable technique. The client in this illustration is a blend of several alcoholics whom the author has treated. The counselor is a directivist. The session is the initial contact.

## Illustration of Recapitulation

CL *Why do I drink? It's easy. No big mystery. My life stinks. I got a boss who's a prick, a wife who's a nag, and five kids that are driving me bananas. That's why I drink. All those tests I took, I could've saved you the trouble. Should've asked me. It would have been simpler. So I got bombed, big deal. Everybody's entitled to once in a while. I did. It's not the first time and it won't be the last. What else have I got? I mean what have I got? I feel like I'm being eaten alive and my bones picked clean. My wife's just not the wife I married. Everytime I turn around it's, Jim, we need this and Jim, we need that. I make a good pay and it's not near enough. I wanted to stop after two kids. She had this crazy idea about big happy families. Well we got a big family all right but it ain't happy lemme tell ya'. Well she learned. Now we don't even sleep in the same bed. Twin beds. I'm in dry dock, nagged to death cause she can't stand her big happy family and blames me besides. Me who never wanted the goddammed kids. No I'm not an alcoholic, I'm too realistic to be an alcoholic. If I'm drinking too much, it's cause my life stinks. That's all. What're you thinkin'?*

CO (Laughs) *I'm thinking that you didn't leave too much out. Your life stinks, a nagging wife, five kids who are driving you crazy, no sex life. You feel like your bones are being picked clean. So you get bombed once in a while. The only thing is you never really finished telling me about your boss. You just said he was a prick and sort of left it at that.*

CL *Like I said, he's a prick. Hounds me. Nags me. In fact he reminds me of my wife and she reminds me of him. Different sexes, same people, and they both get their jollies screwing me. That son-of-a-bitch. You know what that prick does? He comes looking for me in the john. I mean Jesus! I can't even take a crap without worrying about him. People go when they gotta'go and I gotta' go every day about eight. Bastard comes lookin' for me. And I put out more work than anybody on that floor. Everybody knows that, even he knows that, but the bastard will never admit it. Never. Christ who wouldn't drink? I need a couple of quick ones at lunch once in a while. Two days ago I really had it so I didn't come back. I got absolutely stinko. I woke up in detox yesterday morning. So I'm here.*

CO (Nodding) *You said your boss reminds you of your wife. He hounds you like she does. He even comes looking for you in the john even though you put out more work than anybody which he'll never admit. But tell me was it all worth it? Waking up in detox?*

**Comments on Illustrative Excerpt**

The counselor here is building rapport by showing the client he's listening. He lets him vent even more by returning to an undeveloped theme, the boss. By recapitulating so effectively he reinforces the client's understanding.

## ACTIVITIES FOR LEARNING THE TECHNIQUE OF RECAPITULATION

**Justification**

Alcoholism counselors who can recapitulate effectively build rapport, help the client to focus thought, and thereby facilitate the counseling process.

**Purpose**

To develop counselor ability to recapitulate.

**Outcome**

Student counselor is able to incorporate this technique into his/her repertoire of techniques.

**Specific Activities**

1. Verification that student counselor accepts "Justification" previously.

2. Role playing with colleagues, under mentor observation.

3. Role playing with mentor which focuses on recapitulation.

4. Audio tapings with one or more clients.

### Evaluation

1. Feedback from mentor.

2. Activities continue until mentor and student counselor satisfied that skill has been attained.

## CONFRONTATION

### Research

The research indicates that confrontation as a technique is both valuable and productive. In a study by Kaul, Kaul, and Bednar (1973) clients found that confrontation led them to explore their inner feelings.

Kelly (1975) feels that confrontation is more effective and productive than is reflection of feeling. Use of confrontation, he feels, increases self-awareness for both client and counselor and is the technique which most effectively can lead to a client's commitment to change. Koeppen (1972) views confrontation as a threatening technique because pain is given and received but she pointed out, there is a promise to help and grow in this technique too.

### Discussion

The counselor who confronts, threatens. More often than not the alcoholic is scared by confrontation. Why? Because at some level he/she knows that it potentially can tear down defenses and alter not only the distorted perception of self but the perception held of others too. And herein lies the promise to which Koeppen alludes. For only when defenses and perception are righted can the alcoholic get back on the road to recovery.

Confrontation is an art. It's effectiveness will be determined by the counselor's emotional astuteness and competence in discerning the correct moment to confront.

Critical in any confrontation is concern, concern which springs from an honest belief that in the threat of the confrontative remark there does indeed lie a potential for enhancement. The most effective confrontative remarks are those which communicate that concern.

To accomplish this communication the counselor should introduce confrontative questions with words which are neutral and tones which are gentle. For example, with the alcoholic who shows symptoms of **Budding,** the author has found such comments as these following appropriate.

> With the silent alcoholic who's usually talkative. (Chuckle) *"Seems like I've been doing more than my share of talking today. What's happening?"*
>
> With the irritable alcoholic. *"We all have our irritable days, but seems as if you've really been bitten today. Can you tell me about it?"*
>
> With the overconfident, euphoric alcoholic. *"You feel like you're definitely recovered. What do you think that means?"*

The real artistry in the previous confrontative remarks lies in the counselor's ability to have affect gibe with words. The counselor must *be* and *sound* unaffected and must *know* the client. The counselor must feel confident that confrontative remarks will not alienate the client but will indeed enhance the relationship.

## Nondirectivist—Illustrative Excerpt

The following two excerpts illustrate this confrontation technique.

CL *The doctor thinks I ought to go on antabuse.*

CO *Oh? And what's your feeling about that?*

CL *I don't want to.*

CO *You don't want to.*

CL *No.*

(Pause)

CO *You want to tell me why?*

CL *Jesus. If I haven't learned anything else, I've learned I've got do this thing myself. I don't want to get hooked on something and I don't want to lean on any crutch. Besides I don't believe in taking any pills. Like I said I got to do this by myself.*

CO *You don't want to lean on anything or anybody. You want to beat the booze yourself.*

CL *You got it.*

CO (Smiling) *You don't want to lean on anybody. Correct me if I'm wrong but essentially what you're saying is that you don't feel that you need any help.*

CL *I'm not saying that.*

CO *You're not?*

CL *No. There's a difference between leaning and getting help.*

CO (In an honestly bewildered tone) *What's the difference?*

CL *Well, I meant like there's a difference between pills and people. You lean on pills, you get help from people. You're a person I get help from because you're a person.*

CO (Grinning) *Seems like I haven't helped all that much now, have I?*

CL (Grinning back) *You mean just cause I blew it twice in the past month?*

CO (Nodding) *Yeah.* (Pause) *Do you feel the doctor's a person?*

CL *He's okay.*

CO *I guess what you're saying then is that you want my help but not his help.*

CL *No, what I'm saying is I don't want pills.* (Eyes wide) *They're dangerous. They can kill you.*

CO (Nodding) *Or at least make you damn sick if you drink.*

CL (Sheepishly) *Yeah.*

CO *Maybe what you're saying is that you still want to be able to **choose** to get drunk when you want to.*

CL (Stonily) *What I'm saying is that I don't want to get hooked on a pill.*

CO (Grinning) *Are you saying that you prefer to be hooked on alcohol?*

CL (Loudly) *No I'm not saying that.* (Sighing) *Right now I guess I don't know what I'm saying. Let me think about it okay?*

The previous simulated excerpt is an example of the kind of approach to confrontation which this author prefers. The nondirective confronts but does so gently, at times deferentially, but hangs on doggedly, occasionally even dueling intellectually with his/her client in order to adhere to the main point, helping the client to dismantle his/her denial defense and rectify his/her perception.

**Directivist—Illustrative Excerpt**

CL *The doctor thinks I ought to go on antabuse.*

CO *What do you think?*

CL *I don't want to.*

CO *Why not?*

CL *Jesus, if I haven't learned anything else I've learned I've got to do this thing myself. I don't want to get hooked on something and I don't want to lean on any crutch. Besides I don't believe in taking pills. Like I said I got to do this by myself.*

CO *What you're telling me is that you don't think you need any help.*

CL *I'm not saying that.*

CO *So what are you saying?*

CL *There's a difference between leaning and getting help.*

CO (Candidly) *What difference?*

CL *Well, I meant like there's a difference between pills and people. You lean on pills, you get help from people. You're a person. I get help from you because you're a person.*

CO (Seriously) *Doesn't seem like it's been all that much. You got drunk twice in the past month.*

CL *Yeah, but I've been dry now for over a week.*

CO *What are you saying? Maybe that you're not sure you want to stay dry too much longer?*

CL *Christ no! I'm not saying that.*

CO *So what's all this about helping and leaning? Doctors help like they know how, with prescriptions. Me, I help by listening and talking. People help how they can and how they know how. So what are you saying?*

CL (Stonily) *What I'm saying is that I don't want to get hooked on a pill.*

CO (Seriously) *You'd rather be hooked on booze?*

CL *Christ I hope not.*

CO *Okay, let's go over it again . . . .*

This approach is blunt, at times it's almost harsh. There is no intellectual dueling. The counselor's affect is serious and reflective. His/her genuine concern is reflected in final comment, *"Okay, let's go over it again."* What the counselor means is that the client's denial defense needs to be attacked again.

Which of the two approaches is better? It is for the counselor to decide. The most important criterion is that the counselor must be comfortable with the method employed. Directive, nondirective, or somewhere in between, the method must fit with the counselor's personality if he/she is to confront with artistry.

## ACTIVITIES FOR LEARNING THE CONFRONTATION TECHNIQUE

### Justification

Confrontation is conducive to self-exploration and heightened self-awareness by the client. Its especial value in alcoholism counseling is that it can serve as a catalyst to restructure defenses.

### Purpose

To develop the counselor's competence to confront.

### Outcome

Student counselor is able to demonstrate an effective use of confrontation technique.

### Specific Activities

1. Verification that the student counselor accepts and is conversant with the theory behind confrontation.

2. Observation of video tapes or listening to audio tapes of counselors who use this technique effectively.

3. Role playing with colleagues or mentor.

4. Student counselor demonstrates ability to confront with real client (live or on video tape).

**Evaluation**

1. Feedback from mentor.

2. Activities continue until mentor and student counselor are satisfied that skill has been attained.

## SUMMARY

The frame of reference for many alcoholics is derived from the Twelve Steps of A.A. The counselor who has an understanding of these steps finds that rapport comes more easily. Once the counselor has learned how the client interprets these Steps, the counselor gains a valuable window into the client's system of thought and emotional life.

An important task of the counselor is to help the client to redirect and restructure his/her defenses. Explanations and/or illustrations were provided for denial, rationalization, displacement, fantasy, projection, and regression. Repression is a defense better left alone. It's best antidote would seem to be establishment of other defenses like compensation and sublimation.

Silence is threatening even to competent counselors. Silence occurs because of embarrassment, resentments, testing, client conflicts, fear, client need to integrate, and the end of a client-counselor topic. A variety of techniques exist to handle the silence.

The counselor's ability to listen is critically important if progress is going to be made in counseling. He/she needs to listen not only to words but also needs to be exquisitely sensitive to the client's feelings, tones, and sounds. The counselor's motivation to listen is communicated by how he/she sits, by obviating interruptions, by isolating distracting thoughts, by being fully cognizant of those topics and thoughts which can block counselor ability to listen, and by learning to ask focused, pertinent questions.

Questioning as a technique has innate problems because:

—It probes into the unknown.

—Can lead to more questions.

—The client may become conditioned to think in terms of questions and thereby lose his/her sense of responsibility to share more fully in the counseling.

—Counseling focuses upon the cognitive rather than upon feelings. Questioning can also be facilitative as it can lead into productive discussion, especially when the questions are open-ended and avoid the noted dangers.

Reiteration refers to a literal restatement or a rephrasing of what the client says. Reiteration is valuable because it puts the counselor into an accepting role, elicits client feelings, and helps the client to delineate and reconsider his/her thinking.

The counselor who reflects feeling communicates that he/she understands and perceives what the client is feeling and experiencing. Its value lies in helping the client to crystallize his/her feelings and in understanding those feelings in relation to people. When reflecting feeling, the counselor should use simple language and be concerned about timing. This technique enhances the client by helping him/her to learn that feelings cause behavior, that feelings hide feelings. The ultimate benefit of such knowledge is to help the client explore the motives of his/her behavior.

Role playing involves talking, doing, and trying to feel as the other whose role one plays. Role players become the object of their own denials, rationalizations, and projections. It is an especially valuable technique in counseling the alcoholic intrafamilially.

The counselor who recapitulates responds with a focused, succinct synopsis of the client's long monologue. Recapitulation helps the client to build rapport, to focus thoughts, and to keep to a theme. Recapitulation also reinforces the counselor's own understanding.

Confrontation is a valuable and useful technique as has been reported by researchers. The counselor should be fully aware that confrontation can be and often is threatening. Counselors can mitigate this threat if they are emotionally astute, if they know how to discern the correct moment to confront, if they genuinely are concerned and can communicate that concern, and if they introduce their confrontative remarks with neutral words and gentle tones. In addition, they must be and sound unaffected, know their client, and feel confident that their remarks will ultimately enhance the counseling relationship.

## TOPICS FOR DISCUSSION AND REFLECTION

1. With which of the Twelve Steps can you identify the most? Why? With which can you identify the least? Why?

2. Which of the techniques discussed for handling silences do you feel is most effective? Which the least?

3. What are the potential hazards, internal or external which can block effective listening for you?

4. Is it advisable to ask a question which you know will threaten the client? If so, when and under what circumstances?

5. What dangers are there, if any, in reiteration?

6. What merits do you not see in the reflection of feeling technique?

7. What should a counselor's prime concern be when he/she recapitulates?

8. A possible outcome of role playing with a client is counselor self-disclosure. Is this healthy? Unhealthy?

9. Will you be able to confront a client easily? If not, why not?

# REFERENCES


Highlen, P. S., & Baccus, G. K. (1977). Effect of feeling and probe on client self-referenced affect. *Journal of Counseling Psychology, 24* (5) 440-443.

Kaul, T., Kaul, M., & Bednar, R. L. (1973). Counselor confrontation and client depth of self-exploration. *Journal of Counseling Psychology, 20* (2), 3, 132-136.

Kelly, B. J. (1975). Concerned confrontation: The art of counseling. *Social Journal of Educational Research, 9* (3), 110-122.

Koeppen, A. (1972). Confrontation: A threat and a promise. *Texas Personnel and Guidance Journal, 1* (1), 9, 39-43.

Moustakas, C. E. (1966). *The authentic teacher.* Cambridge, MA: Howard A. Doyle Publishing.

Patterson, C. H. (1959). *Counseling and psychotherapy: Theory and practice.* New York: Harper and Row.

Westcott, R. (1966). Introducing coenetics. *American Scholar, 35,* 342-356.

# INDEX

# INDEX

## A



## B

## C

## Q



## R

## S

## T



## U



## V



## W

## Z

# ABOUT THE AUTHOR

# JOSEPH F. PEREZ

The idea for this book finds its roots in a conversation which the author had with his son Christopher who is an alcoholism counselor like his father. Christopher told him that he had not been able to find a text which treats problems peculiar to counseling the alcoholic. He was convinced there was none. The author, who has written several counseling texts, was intrigued. His library researching proved Chris right. There were no books devoted exclusively to alcoholism counseling. And so this text.

Joseph F. Perez is a psychologist, Ph.D., University of Connecticut. His counseling and research with the alcoholic began in 1961 at the Veterans Administration Hospital in Northampton, Massachusetts, and continues today in the college setting and in private practice.

A Professor of Psychology at Westfield State College, Massachusetts, Dr. Perez conducts seminars at both the undergraduate and graduate levels in dynamics of alcoholism and directs workshops for in-service professionals on techniques of counseling the alcoholic. The newest focus of his therapeutic work in alcoholism counseling is facilitating groups with the children of alcoholics. He sees this work as the prime preventive treatment modality of the future. He is now planning a book on the subject. *Counseling the Alcoholic* is the author's ninth professional book. Among his credits he also has a novel, *A Father's Love.*

On the lighter and personal side, Joe Perez loves college teaching because it affords him time for writing, which he describes as a "productive addiction." His other addictions, which he freely admits to, include tennis, cooking (soups, squid, and tripe), and the New York Yankees.

He lives with his wife of thirty years and Mimi, the youngest of their four children, in Northampton, Massachusetts.